THE
WILD WEST

Look-in

THE
WILD WEST

ROBIN MAY

Look-in

Independent Television Books Ltd, London

INDEPENDENT TELEVISION BOOKS LTD.
247 Tottenham Court Road
London W1P 0AU

© Robin May 1975

ISBN 0 900 72731 4

Printed in Great Britain by
Tinling (1973) Ltd, Prescot, Merseyside
(a member of the Oxley Printing Group Ltd.)

Cover photograph: *Wyoming Cowboys* (Wyoming State Archives and Historical Department)

Maps by Jan and John Sandom

For Michael, Elizabeth and David

CONTENTS

INTRODUCTION

A sun-scorched, dusty street at high noon, with two armed men facing each other; the silhouette of a proud Indian brave, motionless against the night sky; a cattle stampede; the cavalry charging to the rescue of a beleaguered wagon train; a grizzled old-timer jumping for joy and shrieking: 'Gold! Gold!'; a saloon brawl brought to an end by a lone, tall man with a star; Custer's Last Stand. . . .

All those moments are part of the West of the cinema, the television screen, and the Western novel, but did it ever really happen like that? Is the story of the Old West more myth than truth?

The answer is yes and no. There were a few gunfights in the best traditions of Hollywood, but far more were sordid affairs in dark alleys or just plain murders. A few lone men did tame towns,

John Wesley Hardin, killer (Rose Collection, U. of Oklahoma Library)

some Indian chiefs were as noble as they looked, real cattle stampedes were more terrifying than any film could ever make them. But there was not much romance in the story of the West, except for the scenery. Instead there was plenty of hardship, pain, sweat, blood, boredom and bravery. No, it was not romantic but it was *epic*. It was *the* American epic.

The Wild West lasted some 350 years, before guts, guns and barbed wire finally brought it to an end. Strictly speaking, though, the Wild West is the era between the end of the great Civil War in 1865 and the late 1890s.

In this book the word 'West' means the vast country of plains, prairies, mountains and deserts across the mighty Mississippi and the wide Missouri, reaching to the Pacific coast. When Americans first explored it at the beginning of the nineteenth century, it consisted—a few Spanish colonies apart—of perhaps a million Indians and countless millions of buffalo, as well as an abundance of wildlife. But to begin the story of the West you must go back as far as 1540. . . .

Doc Holliday, gunfighter and gambler (Kansas State Historical Society)

Jim Bridger, Mountain Man (Kansas State Historical Society)

Wolf Robe, Cheyenne (Smithsonian Institution, National Anthropological Archives)

1
INTO THE UNKNOWN

The Indian hunters, wanderers and farmers who were roaming the West in 1540 had never seen a horse, and hardly any of them had seen a white man. But now the all-conquering, gold-hungry Spaniards, already the masters of Mexico and Peru, had turned their eyes northwards. An expedition was being formed to head from Mexico in search of the Seven Cities of Cibola—the Cities of Gold. There were plenty of volunteers.

The Spaniards had found so much gold in Central and South America that they were prepared to listen to any story about treasure, however far-fetched it was. Such a story had electrified Mexico City in 1536. Some soldiers had come across a white man in rags, with his black servant and some Indians. Weeping with joy, the white man said that his name was de Vaca, that he was the sole survivor of an expedition to Florida in the extreme Southeast of what is now the United States, and that he had not seen another white man for eight years.

He babbled away about treasure, but he seemed to be holding back some secret. Did he want to tell the Spanish king personally about what he had seen, or head northwards again himself? The Viceroy, who ruled Mexico for the king, sent a friar called Marcos de Niza north to check the story, and with him went de Vaca's black servant, Estevan.

When the friar returned he brought thrilling news. He had seen the golden city, the magic city of Cibola, he told anyone who cared to listen, which meant the entire population of Mexico City. Even when he confessed that he had only seen Cibola at a distance, nobody's gold fever seemed in any way diminished. But where was Estevan, he was asked? Dead, it appeared, but not before he had visited the wonderful place, which consisted of no less than seven cities, paved in gold, silver and turquoises.

An expedition complete with artillery and horses was rapidly mounted, several thousand Spaniards setting out in March 1540, along with hundreds of Mexicans and Indians, and Friar Marcos de Niza. The commander was a tough Spanish noble, Francisco de Coronado.

After a rugged march of some 1,600 kilometres they reached and stormed Cibola. But where was all the gold and silver? From a distance the cities looked like palaces in the fierce sun, but, close to, Cibola turned out to be one of seven Indian villages of houses made of mud and stone, some of them four storeys high. De Niza had let his imagination run away with him.

He was lucky not to be hanged, merely being sent back to Mexico in disgrace. Fortunately, Cibola was full of supplies, and when Coronado's men had rested, they pressed on. Still hoping for gold, they believed an Indian who claimed he had seen a place where little golden bells hung on trees, but when he failed to lead the Spaniards there he was strangled.

The expedition returned to Mexico in 1542 and Coronado was branded a failure. Yet he had triumphed, geographically at least, for he and his men had gone as far north as Kansas and eastwards into Oklahoma and Texas, as they were later to be called. They had gazed in wonder at the Grand Canyon and seen endless herds of buffalo. Only a third of them had survived, but they had discovered the West.

They left a legacy behind them, for some of their horses remained, from which stemmed the wild horses of the American Plains. Within a few generations the mounted Plains Indian was born.

An Empire under Attack

Not until the early eighteenth century did the Spaniards make any real attempt to follow up Coronado's bold expedition. By the time they began to build a string of missions, ranches and villages right across what is now the southern border of the United States from Florida to California, the tribes of the Southwest had become superb horsemen. The Comanches, later to be known as the 'Lords of the South Plains', played havoc with Spanish missions in the 1750s, helped by French arms, for by now French explorers had penetrated deep into the West from Canada. And the Apaches, too, joined in the attacks on Spanish outposts in the Southwest, until the order went out from Mexico: 'Exterminate the Apaches!' It was easier said than done.

Only in the Far West did Spain have any success, for there dedicated priests established good relations with the less warlike Indians of California; but, meanwhile, Spain's attention was drawn back to Europe. While Britain gained Canada from France in the 1760s, then lost her American colonies in the 1770s, the Spanish possessions in America, such as they were, stagnated. So that when the first American reached the West in 1804, Spain's influence, except in California and the extreme Southwest, was almost nil.

Yet even today traces of Spain survive in innumerable place names (El Paso, San Francisco, Los Angeles etc.), in Mexican-American costume and cowboy gear, and in language. Many American words are adapted from the Spanish, like ranch from *rancho*, and others are still as they were, like rodeo. And the Spaniards brought cattle as well as the horse to America, also orange and lemon trees and much magnificent architecture which can still be seen in the Southwest and California.

Americans in the West

While Spain was keeping its foothold in the West, the French had acquired Louisiana, which then consisted of the whole Mississippi Valley to the Rocky Mountains. In 1803 the American President, Thomas Jefferson, bought this colossal area from the French (who knew next to nothing about it beyond what a few explorers had found) for a mere $15 million. Overnight the young United States doubled in size. It was the best land deal in history.

Into this unknown land Jefferson sent Captain Meriwether Lewis and his friend Lieutenant William Clark with orders to explore the Missouri River and, if possible, find a water route to the Pacific. They were to note all the flora and fauna on the way and study the way of life of the various Indian tribes.

On 14 May, 1804 they 'hoisted Sail and set out out in high spirits for the Western Expedition'. They made the difficult trip up the Missouri and reached a point near what is now Bismarck,

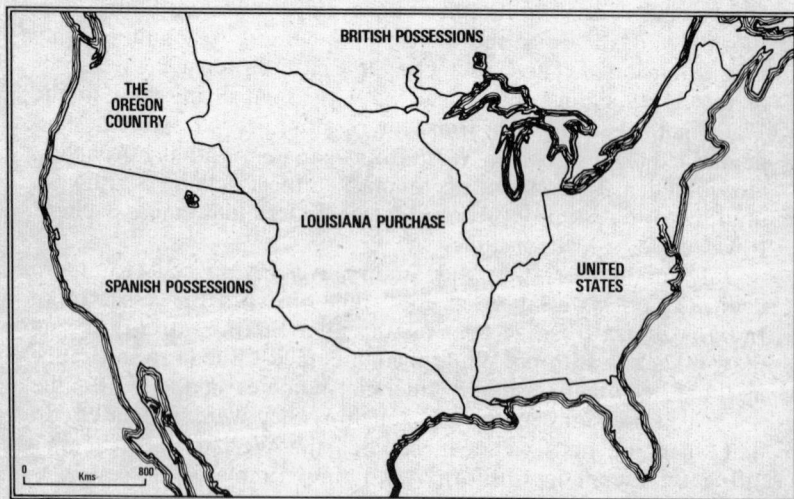

BRITISH POSSESSIONS

THE OREGON COUNTRY

LOUISIANA PURCHASE

SPANISH POSSESSIONS

UNITED STATES

0   Kms   800

North Dakota, where they spent the winter among the very intelligent Mandan Indians.

Unlike later travellers, Lewis, Clark and their men befriended the Indians, many of whom had not seen white men before, and they had only minor problems with them. Amazingly, of the thirty-two people who set out from winter quarters in the spring of 1805, all returned safely. The only casualty was a soldier who had died earlier of appendicitis.

It was in winter quarters that a young Shoshone Indian girl called Sacajawea, and her French-Canadian husband, joined the expedition. She was invaluable to Lewis and Clark, guiding the party and acting as an interpreter when they reached her homeland high in the Rockies. Only about 18, Sacajawea carried a baby thousands of miles on her back. The sight of an Indian girl and a child with the expedition convinced watching Indians that the expedition was a peaceful one.

It was not all smooth going. Near the Falls of the Missouri, Lewis ran into an ugly customer. It was 14 June, 1805; and a large brown bear crept up on him.

I drew up my gun to shoot . . . she was not loaded. I ran hastily into the water. . . . It now seemed to me that all the beasts of the neighbourhood had made a league to destroy me. . . .

Lewis was only exaggerating a little, for he was first attacked by a cougar or a wolverine, then, having driven that off with a shot, was charged by three bull buffaloes. Luckily, the buffaloes suddenly changed their minds.

Sacajawea's people, the Shoshones, helped Lewis and Clark all they could, and though no direct water route to the Pacific was found, they reached the mouth of the Columbia River on 7 November, 1805 and spent a cold, wet winter on the Pacific coast in a fort they built there. On the way back Lewis and clark split the expedition to explore the territory more fully, met each other again, and arrived safely at St. Louis in September 1806. They had come back with a huge fund of information and had treated the Indians honourably in the main.

There were two other interesting and unusual characters besides Sacajawea on the Lewis and Clark expedition: Clark's black slave York, who made a great hit with Indian ladies on the journey, and, almost as large as the huge black, Lewis's Newfoundland dog Scannon. The whole adventure made a comparatively peaceful start to the violent years that followed.

What happened to Clark's black slave York after the expedition?
Clark freed him. He had been popular with the party and the Indians. Not only was he very strong, but he was such good company. He became a drayman, carrying drink between Nashville, Tennessee, and Richmond, Kentucky. But his favourite occupation, like many Westerners of his day, was telling taller and taller stories.

Is more known about Lewis's dog Scannon?
This splendid Newfoundland had his own adventures on the trail. He was much admired by the Indians, who kept making offers for him. Lewis had paid $20 for him and wasn't selling. Once, some Indians stole him and three men were sent to get him back. They came upon the thieves who fled, leaving Scannon behind.

What happened to Lewis and Clark after their great expedition?
Lewis was made Governor of Louisiana Territory, but was not very good at the job, and began brooding about himself and his health. In 1809 he died mysteriously in Tennessee, murdered perhaps, or killed by his own hand.

Clark had a happier life. He became Governor of Missouri Territory, then Superintendent of Indian Affairs, and he had Sacajawea's three children educated. He was one of the few whites whom the Indians loved.

Their journals first appeared in print in 1814, by which time Lewis was dead.

2
TRAPPERS AND
TRAILBLAZERS

It was an autumn day in 1808 in what is now the state of Montana, and John Colter was running for his life. The rugged young fur trapper had been captured by a war party of some 500 Blackfeet, after his partner, John Potts, had tried to resist and been killed by a shower of arrows through his body. Both had been with Lewis and Clark two years earlier.

The Blackfeet, the dreaded 'raiders of the Northwestern Plains', had come to distrust white interlopers especially after one was seen fighting with the Crows against the Blackfeet. Now Colter was to pay for the 'crimes' of others. Stripped and shoeless he stood waiting to die. He could see that the war party's leaders were discussing him, then one came up to him and asked him how fast he could run. 'I'm a terrible runner, as slow as a turtle', he lied, whereupon he was told to save himself if he could—over ground covered with prickly-pear thorns and rocks. He set off at the double with a thirty-second start.

The human turtle proved to be an antelope, as his hunters, spears at

'The Trapper's Last Shot'—a Mountain Man in a desperate situation with Indians closing in on him (Missouri Historical Society)

15

the ready, soon found. Colter knew he had to reach the Madison River, some nine kilometres away, and after five kilometres he had outstripped all but one of his pursuers. Instant action was needed. He swung round, tripped the Indian up, then killed him with his fallen spear.

Colter ran on and at last reached the river, plunged into its icy waters and swam to some driftwood under which he hid, while furious Blackfeet roamed the bank searching for him. Finally, they gave up, and that night he swam several kilometres downstream, clambered ashore and started to run, then walk, then stagger towards his base camp over 300 kilometres away. He arrived there a week later to the amazement of his friends who saw a bloodstained, wild-eyed, starving apparition in front of them. Yet after only a few weeks, Colter was fit again, his torn feet healed, and he was raring to get back to work.

Colter, the first white man to see the wonders of Yellowstone Park, is usually regarded as the original Mountain Man. Despite their nickname Mountain Men were not mountaineers, unless a mountain, an obstacle to be avoided or crossed in their search for beaver, happened to be in their way. They would go anywhere to trap beaver because its fur was so valuable. Around 1810 it became high fashion in Europe and America for men to wear beaver hats and to have beaver collars on their capes; ladies, too, liked beaver-fur trimmings. By 1813 the trade was booming in the West, not only on American soil but to the north where the Hudson's Bay Company, founded two centuries earlier, had spread its tentacles across to the Pacific coast.

The Mountain Men were mostly Americans of British descent, though there were Britons and French Canadians in the trade, as well as Mexicans and some blacks. Their gaudy glory days ended around 1840, when beaver fur became unfashionable. By that time these white men, who lived like the Indians they traded with, fought, befriended and married, had blazed trails right across the West—over deserts, mountains, across great plains and through forests.

Young Men Wanted

The Mountain Men era reached its peak one day in 1822 when a Colonel Ashley advertised in a St. Louis, Missouri, newspaper. Some of those concerned had to get friends to read the advertisement out, for many Mountain Men could not read or write. It was to help transform America:

> TO Enterprising Young Men: The subscriber wishes to engage ONE HUNDRED MEN, to ascend the river Missouri to its source, there to be employed for one, two or three years. . . .

Some of the adventurous young and not so young men who answered the call were to become legends: men like Jedediah Smith, young Jim Bridger (who had to get someone to read the advertisement) and, later, Kit Carson. These and others like them criss-crossed the West with their trails.

The Mountain Men were an independent bunch. Some hired themselves out, others preferred working alone or in small bands after they had done their time with Ashley. He needed them to combat not only wild Indians but the influence of British traders and trappers from Canada in what the Americans now considered *their* Northwest, and he got all the men he asked for. One of the greatest was Jedediah Smith, a religious and sober man unlike most of his friends. He pioneered the route to California, survived terrible journeys through some of the worst deserts in the world, and battled with both Indians and grizzlies, until in 1831, aged only thirty-two, he fell under a Comanche lance.

Jim Bridger, for all that he could neither read nor write, could speak ten Indian languages and Spanish. No one has ever known the West as well as Jim. In unknown country he regularly looked behind him on the trail, as well as forwards and sideways, a tip that is still useful today in town and country alike.

He had plenty of bright ideas. Mountain Men often shared their clothes with countless vermin on long trips on the trail. Jim dry-cleaned his buckskins over an ant-hill. He was the first white man to see the Great Salt Lake and taste its bitter waters, and he fought and survived innumerable fights and skirmishes with Indians. Unlike many of his friends and enemies, he survived the end of the fur trade, living on for almost half a century, having been a scout, guide and trader.

Glass and the Grizzly

No one is quite sure about Old Hugh Glass. Assuming that his legend is part fact, when he was in his sixties, an age rarely reached by any early inhabitant of the West, he was deserted by two friends after coming off a poor second in an encounter with a grizzly. Feeling rather hard done by, he set off on a 320-kilometre crawl to get his revenge. He caught up with the first false friend and forgave him because he was young, but continued searching for the other one, finally catching up with him, only to find—to his intense disgust— that he could not touch him because he had joined the army. Presumably the two deserters had seen the old man's wounds and written him off as a goner. They were wrong: no Mountain Man could ever be written off until he was chopped into little pieces, though some grizzled old liar would be around to say that he'd seen the pieces of some hard case come together again!

Every summer Mountain Men would assemble at a pre-arranged rendezvous camp often high in the Rocky Mountains. There they would trade, swop tall stories, drink, fight, gamble, race their horses, marry Indian women, and fight some more. Every night gusts of merry laughter would ring round the camp.

The various fur companies sent agents to the camps with goods, money and tools to exchange for the beaver skins and the skins of other fur-bearing animals. The Mountain Men made small fortunes—which many of them promptly lost in huge gambling sprees before going back to work. As the fur trade started to collapse, the rendezvous camps began to get smaller, and the wiser Mountain Men started thinking about the future. Few headed East to settle down. They weren't cut out to be farmers. Scouting, guiding wagon trains westwards or leading parties of explorers might not be the same as trapping with boon companions or alone several hundred miles from the nearest outposts of 'civilisation'—such as Fort Laramie or Bent's Fort—but at least wielding a muzzle-loader or a knife was more like man's work than heading East and wielding a plough.

In fact the trade in beaver stopped just in time, for except in Canada, the animal was almost extinct in many areas from over-trapping.

How many Mountain Men were there?
Even in their greatest days there can never have been more than 500 working in a single year. Perhaps there were 2,000 in all.

What did Mountain Man John Hatcher mean when he said: 'A little 'bacca, ef its a plew a plug, an' Dupont an' Galena, a Green River or so, an' he leaves for the Bayou Salade?'
Yes, Mountain Men did use rather obscure slang! Translated, Hatcher's speech reads, 'A little tobacco, even if it costs a beaver skin a plug, and some gunpowder and lead, and a hunting knife or so, and he leaves for the trapping country Mountain Men call the Bayou Salade.' A plew? It comes from the French-Canadian word for 'hairy'—*pélu*. 'Galena' is a mining term, being a sulphide of lead that contains silver. It became the trappers' name for the lead that they used to make their own bullets. As for 'Dupont', the firm of Dupont manufactured gunpowder. And a 'Green River'? That was a trapper's hunting knife made at Green River, Wyoming. The Bayou Salade was a spot in the Colorado Rockies, the words meaning 'salt marsh' in trapper language. There was salt rock in the area.

3
WESTWARD THE WAGONS

Shouts and roars of laughter split the air, whips cracked and
wagons creaked, and night and day the noise never ceased. But
above it all was the sound of hammers beating down endlessly on
anvils as blacksmiths in some twenty workshops repaired and got
ready covered wagons for the 3,200 kilometre journey to Oregon.
The place was Independence, Missouri, any time in the 1840s.
Its streets were thronged with mules, oxen and horses and a
seething mass of humanity. Independence was one of several
starting points and the most important of them for all that it had
a mere 1,600 inhabitants. It also had thirty stores, two hotels and
many boarding houses, and Oregon fever burned bright in every
one of them. There were storekeepers looking prosperous, as well
they might from the fortunes they were making from the emigrants. There were Spanish traders, flint-eyed gamblers dressed in
the height of fashion, Indians, and Mountain Men. And there
were the emigrants, men, women and children of all ages pre-
paring to head for Oregon in the distant Northwest, the Promised
Land of Oregon which was said to be fertile beyond belief. They
were prepared to face every obstacle, human and physical, to
reach their destination and settle down. They were America on the
move.

Concordia, Kansas, 'town' to settlers in 1870 (Kansas State Historical Soc.)

Independence was the start of three immortal trails, the Oregon, the California and the Santa Fe, all blazed by Mountain Men.

The Santa Fe was a trading, not an emigrant, route and had been in use by traders since the 1820s, despite constant attacks by the fierce Comanches and Kiowas on the traders and trappers who ventured along it. The California Trail followed the Oregon Trail as far as Fort Hall, Idaho, then swung west. It did not come into its own until the Gold Rush of 1849, the year after gold was found in California, by which time the perils of the Oregon Trail had gripped the imagination of the world.

Mountain Men had passed along the Oregon Trail before it was an official route, but what made ordinary folk risk their lives crossing plains, mountains and raging torrents, risking death by thirst, disease, hunger, drowning, exhaustion and Indian arrows? No one has ever really solved the mystery of why these restless folk set out, but a few of their reasons are plain enough. Early white visitors to the Oregon country, including the Reverend Jason Lee, who started a mission in the Willamette Valley, discovered a fertile paradise ready for settlement. Lee returned east to lecture about his valley until it seemed like the Promised Land and an earthly paradise rolled into one.

Politicians and newspapers preached Oregon to the masses, because the United States and Britain were hotly disputing the ownership of the great Northwest. If enough Americans crossed to Oregon it would become American by right of occupation. Congress, the American governing body, had offered 270 hectares to every man who settled in Oregon, plus 65 hectares for his wife and the same for every child. As land everywhere else had to be grabbed or bought, this was a sensational offer. No wonder they wrote 'Oregon—or Bust' on their wagons. So the call went out and Oregon fever spread like a raging prairie fire. It became a crusade, made all the greater by the wanderlust which drove the Frontier people of America further and further west. Some instinct drove them on, part adventure, part curiosity, part land hunger. Their ancestors and fathers and grandparents had headed west, but a few kilometres at a time. Now they were prepared to take a giant 3,000 kilometre step from the Mississippi-Missouri frontier to the Pacific itself.

The Great Emigration

The first group crossed in 1841, but it was the 'Great Emigration' of 1843 which set the pattern and solved the question of who owned Oregon by filling the area with Americans. A treaty in 1846

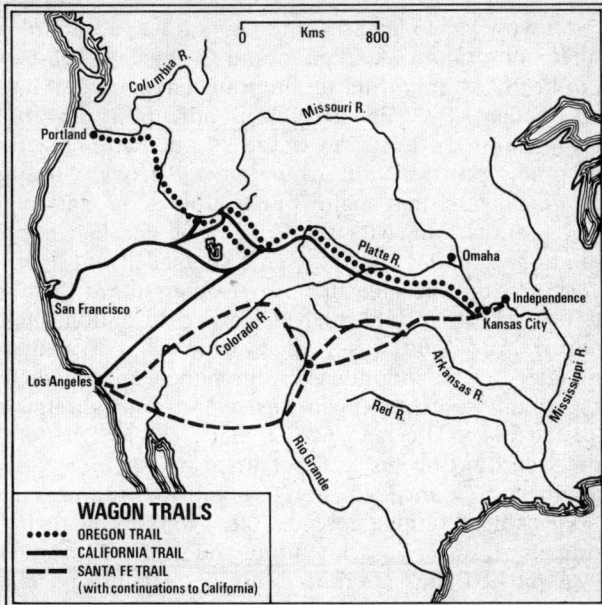

WAGON TRAILS
••••• OREGON TRAIL
——— CALIFORNIA TRAIL
– – – SANTA FE TRAIL
(with continuations to California)

confirmed American right to the area, and the border between Canada and America became the 49th Parallel. True, only some 10,000 settled in Oregon in the 1840s, compared to the hundreds of thousands who hit the California Trail seeking gold after 1848, but those 10,000 were the history-makers who survived the greatest mass trek in history.

Some 200 families and other emigrants, 1,000 strong, assembled on 18 May, 1843 a few kilometres from Independence, knowing that Oregon had to be reached before winter. Those with families travelled in canvas-covered wagons, many of which were ordinary farm wagons about three metres by one metre. Buckets were hung under these box-like carts, also water kegs, lanterns, tools and a churn, while inside were clothes, pots, pans, rifles etc. Bedding had somehow to be fitted on the crowded floor. The better-off families usually had two wagons.

The wagons were mostly dragged by oxen, for it was soon found that these were stronger and more dependable than mules or horses. So the emigrants headed for the rendezvous through the last outposts of civilisation, the men driving their cattle (5,000 headed west with the emigrants) while the women and children walked beside their moving homes. It was noted by watchers how smart everyone looked. That would all change in the months to come.

The pilot who was to lead them to Oregon was an old Mountain Man called John Gantt. A Captain and Council of Ten were also elected to keep law and order on the trail. Then, on 22 May, came the great moment. The pilot stood in his stirrups at sun-up, waved his hat and pointed west. They made 24 kilometres the first day through green prairie, and camped by a grove. Singing and laughter were heard that night, but trouble soon started. It was caused by bad discipline, for the Council of Ten had not got the wilder emigrants under control. Some slugged it out over water-holes to show what big men they were, others raced their wagons to show off, still more had not yet learned to handle their half-tamed oxen. And food was wasted, which was to cause much suffering later. In the end, however, the punch-up brigade learned their lesson and stuck to cussin' instead of fist-fighting. As one emigrant recalled: 'The man with a black eye and battered face could not well hunt up his cattle or drive his team.'

Gradually the Council got things organised, setting men with special skills—blacksmiths, cobblers etc.—to work at their trades, and fixing guard rosters, stock tending and sanitary arrangements. Camp was pitched each afternoon and the wagons put in a circle for protection, though Indians never attacked a wagon train in the 1840s on the Oregon Trail, whatever films claim to the contrary. The attacks came later, when land grabs and massacres by both sides inflamed racial hatred.

After walking on that first day, women and children tended to stay in the wagons, the men and boys riding alongside, though in eastern Kansas the women often walked through the wild flowers along the route for sheer enjoyment. The pilot, aiming at a steady 19 kilometres a day, would be out in front of the kilometre-long column looking for the next camping ground, or for fords over streams and small rivers. The first difficult river crossing, across the Kansas, took several days. The emigrants used rafts and Indian 'bull boats', wooden frames with buffalo hides stretched across them.

There were plenty of Indians about now, often in war paint, so Gantt ordered that they should be given a few cattle, or they would steal them.

The lush vegetation was beginning to disappear, but there was plenty of animal life to enjoy—antelope, rabbits, prairie dogs and sometimes great herds of buffalo. With trees growing scarce, then becoming almost non-existent, the travellers used 'buffalo chips' (dried buffalo dung) as fuel.

By now those without cattle were starting to resent helping to look after them, so the train was split into two, the Cow Column following the rest. The wagons were chained together overnight to stop oxen breaking out and Indians—if any—breaking in. Breakfast began at six and ended at seven. Those not ready to move out might find themselves at the back of the column eating dust all day, though everyone in theory took turns at the rear. By now the women were longing to have a real laundry day, while many of the babies were suffering from nappy rash. Each noon there was a halt, when the Council met, then on the wagon train pressed until mid-afternoon. Stragglers could then catch up—or be left behind. Oregon had to be reached before the winter. One California-bound wagon train was trapped in the mountains and those that lived through the nightmare in the snows only survived by resorting to cannibalism.

They reached the Platte River on 29 June. It was a mile wide and an inch deep, or so the humorous writer, Mark Twain, claimed. Another comedian said that the river was 'too thick to drink and to thin to plough.' The trouble was that it could be extremely treacherous in places with a bottom like a 'shifty quicksand', and wagons could get hopelessly stuck in the sand. The 1843 expedition took six days to cross the river, making rafts out of their wagon box tops by sewing buffalo hides together and

A wagon train crossing the Smoky Hill River in 1867 (Kansas State Hist. Soc.)

stretching them across the tops. The sun soon dried the hides and the rafts carried goods, wives and children across. A chain extended the full length of the train to keep the teams in a straight line and together.

After the crossing the landscape became drier and sandier, and many of the wagons needed repairing. On 14 July, the wagon train reached Fort Laramie and the women had a chance to do some washing. The famous fur-trading post had an Indian camp nearby for the children to stare at, while the Indians imagined that a whole tribe of whites was on the march, having no idea of the millions of Americans still in the East.

After two days, the emigrants set out again and the going got harder and harder. However, they had restocked their food supplies and had had a chance to repair their wagons, but now the oxen were getting steadily weaker, and too many of the springs had foul water. A few years after the Great Emigration this section of the march was littered with abandoned wheels, broken tools and utensils, and graves.

Suddenly, they were over the backbone of the continent and the rivers were flowing westwards. After days that seemed longer and longer they reached Fort Hall, only to find that the most dangerous part of their journey was about to begin. The last 800 kilometres were to be the toughest.

Some of this part of the journey was nightmarish.

One horrifying stretch was the Devil's Backbone. The wagons inched along a narrow ridge over a kilometre and a half long, with a 300-metre gorge on their left and a steep precipice down to the foaming Snake River on the right. No one dared ride in a wagon. Miraculously, they all survived.

On 16 October, the party split into two, some pressing on through tortuous gorges and across mountain ranges, the rest taking to the rivers. Later travellers found an easier route, but in 1843 both groups suffered greatly. Those who went by land finally reached the Willamette Valley in a state of utter exhaustion.

But some of those who took to the rivers never reached the Promised Land at all. It was the mighty Columbia River which was to be the death of them. At Fort Walla Walla the emigrants were befriended by the employees of the Hudson's Bay post, and they rested, then built themselves small craft which could carry eight to ten people. Their wagons and cattle were left at the fort to be reclaimed later—if they survived. There were 320 kilometres to go.

On 1 November, the fleet of little boats set out, surging safely

Settlers in front of their sod house in Nebraska in the late 1880s (Nebraska State His. Soc.)

through the rapids that they met. Young Jesse Applegate was in the leading boat and very excited, if somewhat alarmed. It was piloted by an Indian with a red band round his long hair.

Suddenly, Jesse saw a smaller boat near the other bank in which were five people, including his brother and two young cousins. All at once, the distant boat struck a rock:

> The boat we were watching disappeared and we saw the men and boys struggling in the water. Father and Uncle Jesse, seeing their children drowning, were seized with frenzy, and dropping their oars, sprang up from their seats and were about to leap from the boat to make a desperate attempt to swim to them, when mother and Aunt Cynthia, in voices that were distinctly heard above the roar of the rushing waters, by commands and entreaties brought them to a realisation of our own perilous situation, and the madness of an attempt to reach the other side by swimming.

Jesse's brother and one other were saved by being washed on to a small island linked to the shore by a thin causeway. There was one other survivor, but both Jesse's cousins drowned.

At last, in small groups, the boats reached Fort Vancouver (not to be confused with Vancouver in Canada). It was now late autumn and rain was falling steadily. Was this the Promised Land that they had come 3,200 kilometres to find?

They rowed to the mouth of the Willamette River and reached the valley of their dreams. There was much work to be done before winter finally closed in, but the huge fir trees made superb fence rails and were easy to split. And to their amazement the emigrants found that wheat could be planted at once and would grow in the winter.

In parts of the West the ruts made by the wagon wheels on the Oregon Trail can be seen to this day.

March of the Mormons

There was one trail to the West that was like no other. Most of those who headed westwards wanted land, gold or adventure, some of them all three. This was not the case with the religious sect known as the Mormons. All they sought was freedom to worship as they pleased.

The sect had been founded in New York State in 1830 by Joseph Smith, whose Church of Jesus Christ of Latter Day Saints believed in the Book of Mormon. The first Mormon home was in Ohio, but their neighbours forced them to flee to Missouri where

Brigham Young, Mormon extraordinary (Utah State His. Soc.)

their life-style, success, and hostility to slavery in an area which supported it, led to riots against them. They set out for Illinois and established Nauvoo on the Mississippi River.

Alas, their leader asked for trouble and got it. He believed that his people were above local law, then announced that one man could have several wives. This not only split the Mormons but aroused the wrath of everyone else. He was murdered by a mob in 1843, but there was a greater man ready to take his place, the extraordinary Brigham Young. Young was a veritable Moses of his people, leading them to safety and settling them even further west in Nebraska.

But it was still not far enough from their enemies, so early in 1847 he led an advance party to Salt Lake Valley, Utah. He looked at the valley and said simply: 'This is the place.' His followers were planting crops the very next day.

Word was sent back to the waiting Mormons and thousands crossed the plains eager 'to make the desert bloom'. Yet it appeared that they were doomed from the start, for the spring crops were threatened by millions of grasshoppers, who fell on the wheat and began devouring it. When all seemed lost a miracle suddenly occurred, for from the lake there rose up clouds of seagulls who ate the grasshoppers, which are now known as Mormon crickets. Soon the desert was blooming indeed.

Converts began flocking to Salt Lake City from the Eastern states and from Europe, especially the industrial slums of Britain. In 1849, Young had another brilliant idea. He announced that the newcomers should cross the plains to Utah pulling handcarts holding up to 225 kilos of belongings. Over 3,000 made the long journey in this way during the next four years, walking around 50 kilometres a day, twice as fast as the oxen of the Oregon Trail could manage. But even in the wilderness the Mormons found themselves hated, partly because of their many wives, partly because they were 'different': they tried to get on with Indians, they were not interested in gold. Brigham Young said it was for paving streets!

Utah did not become a state until 1896, after the law allowing many wives had been abolished. Young himself died in 1877, leaving a fortune of more than two million dollars to his seventeen wives and fifty-six children!

The Santa Fe Trail

There were few saints on the Santa Fe Trail but plenty of sinners of all races. Trading and fighting were its specialities. From the 1820s Americans transported goods to Santa Fe and returned to Missouri with precious metals and furs. Great caravans went up and down the trail, the wagons being far more splendid than those that had headed for Oregon, and in 1846 one caravan had set out with no less than 400 wagons. In that year the United States went to war with Mexico, so the Santa Fe Trail became a military road as well. After the war was over, with tension rising between Indians and Americans, the route became a trail of tears and blood, of fear and sudden death. Not until the Comanches were finally subdued in the 1870s was the trail really safe.

Gone to Texas!

Texas had received its first flood of American settlers as far back as the 1820s and 1830s. But especially after Texas became independent of Mexico in 1836, settlers in their thousands, mainly from the South, headed there. Often, they wrote GTT on their houses and shacks—Gone to Texas—just in case anyone was in any doubt as to where they had gone. Most of them travelled rough, though the richer ones managed it in style and comfort aboard steamboats.

The first American families reached Texas in 1821, after Mexico broke away from Spanish rule. Three hundred families, led by a young lawyer named Stephen Austin, settled there with the blessing of the new regime, but from the outset their different ways annoyed the government in Mexico City.

The crisis came in 1833 when a dictator named Santa Anna became President of Mexico. He had no time for the Americans, who prepared to rebel to gain their independence. By 1836 there were 30,000 of them in Texas and only 7,000 Mexicans. So it was hardly surprising that the Texans did well at first, well enough for a furious Santa Anna to head north from Mexico to punish them. Texas promptly declared itself independent, its troops being given to a larger-than-life character to command, Sam Houston. This ex-governor of Tennessee, who was to become the first President of Texas, was the right man to take control in a desperate crisis. He was also, incidentally, one of the few Texans who actually liked Indians, being a blood brother of the Cherokees.

After a forced march, Santa Anna closed in on a mission hastily turned into a fortress at San Antonio. It was called the Alamo.

Now a Texan shrine, it was defended from 23 February to 6 March 1836 by some 180 heroes against a Mexican army of 4,000.

Sam Houston, saviour of Texas (Library of Congress)

In command of the Alamo were three men: William B. Travis, a fiery young lawyer, Davy Crockett, backwoodsman, politician and teller of tall tales, and Jim Bowie of knife fame. Travis sent out an appeal for help which reads like a battle cry;

> TO THE PEOPLE OF TEXAS AND ALL AMERICANS IN THE WORLD Fellow Citizens and Compatriots: I am besieged by a thousand or more Mexicans under Santa Anna. I have sustained a continual bombardment for twenty-four hours and have not lost a man. The enemy have demanded surrender at discretion; otherwise the garrison is to be put to the sword if the place is taken. I have answered the summons with a cannon shot and our flag still waves proudly from the walls. I shall never surrender or retreat. Then I call upon you, in the name of liberty, of patriotism, and of everything dear to the American character, to come to our aid with all dispatch. The enemy are receiving reinforcements daily . . . I am determined to sustain myself as long as possible and die like a soldier who never forgets what is due to his honour or that of his country —VICTORY OR DEATH.

The restored chapel of the Alamo, the most honoured spot in Texas (Author's collection)

All the valiant garrison died and hundreds of Mexicans too: then, out of the shambles that was the Alamo came fifteen women and children. The slaughtered defenders had done their job well, for they had given Texas time, time to survive.

Having taken the Alamo, Santa Anna turned to butchery, ordering that some three hundred Texans who had surrendered to a Mexican force at Goliad should be murdered to a man.

The Texas army was now only eight hundred strong and was in full retreat. But Houston's luck was about to change. In April 1836 at San Jacinto, Santa Anna was so over-confident that he let the Texans surprise him. In a vicious battle lasting only twenty minutes he was utterly defeated by Texans shouting their new battle cry: 'Remember the Alamo!' Six hundred Mexicans lay dead and Santa Anna was captured. The Texans lost only nine men.

In September 1836, Sam Houston was elected President of Texas. And in 1847, he achieved his heart's desire, the entry of Texas into the United States. The long delay had been caused because Texas was a slave-owning state, and there were many Northerners, finally overruled, who had no desire for another slave state to be added to the Union. Sadly, Sam Houston, who became governor of the state of Texas, had to retire from public life in 1861, because when the Civil War between North and South broke out over states' rights and the slavery question, Texas sided with the South, the Confederacy, and Sam was a firm Union man who believed in a united America.

But the war that dramatically changed the West was the campaign by the United States against Mexico (1846-8) which gave the Americans most of Arizona and New Mexico, and the supreme prize, California.

Not that anyone realised California's value until suddenly something exciting happened just before the final peace treaty was signed, something that was to change the history of California and the whole United States. A man named Marshall had found gold.

Did anyone escape from the Alamo?
Besides the handful of women and children, there is strong evidence that one man, Moses Rose, escaped before the final assault. It is to be hoped that he really did, for he later told one of the grandest of all Texas tales. Travis assembled the garrison, told them there was no hope of outside help, said that he would remain to die, and offered everyone the chance to escape or to cross a line that he drew with his sword on the ground. If they crossed the line, it meant they would die with him. All crossed except Rose, who climbed the walls to relate his story years later. Even Jim Bowie, lying in a cot near death from pneumonia, and with a badly smashed hip, crossed the line. 'Boys,' he asked, 'will some of you kindly lift my cot across?' And they did. He may have been the last to die, sitting up in his cot in the baptistry of the Alamo church, and killing an unknown number of Mexicans with his four pistols and famous knife before he was overwhelmed.

4
GOLD FEVER

Madness was in the air. It had overtaken the inhabitants of the tiny town of San Francisco in May 1848, after a wild-eyed man had rushed down the main street shouting: 'Gold! Gold! Gold from the American River!' and brandishing a bottle containing precious gold dust above his head. By June mere madness was turning to insanity, as one of the afflicted later described:

> The excitement produced was intense; and many were soon busy in their hasty preparations for a departure for the mines. The family who had kept house for me caught the moving infection. Husband and wife were both packing up; the blacksmith dropped his hammer, the carpenter his plane, the mason his trowel, the farmer his sickle, the baker his loaf, and the tapster his bottle. All were off to the mines, some on carts, some on horses, and some on crutches, and one went in a litter.

So began the biggest bonanza ever, the greatest gold rush in history. But news and people travelled slower then, so it was not until 1849 that the world-wide stampede to California got under way. The stampeders were nicknamed the 'Forty-Niners'.

The Californian Gold Rush started a pattern that repeated itself for fifty years, in other parts of the West, in Australia, in New Zealand, in South Africa and, finally, in the fabulous Klondike Stampede of 1898 to a spot in the distant Northwest of Canada near the Alaskan border.

The pattern was always the same. First came news of the strike, then the rush began. Whole ships' crews deserted and headed for the goldfields, office boys all over America, in Britain, in Europe, left their desks at the double and headed for the docks. Every sort of man from killers to the most sober, upright citizens, hit the trail, and just a few found wealth beyond their dreams. Far more found a little or no gold, while many never arrived at all.

So great was the lure of gold that some old men who took part in the Klondike Stampede of '98 had been in California, and in Australia and New Zealand too!

The discovery of gold had come on 24 January 1848. Only five years later some 250 million dollars' worth of gold had already been found.

The strike occurred during the building of a saw mill on land belonging to an adventurous businessman and settler from Switzerland called John Sutter. His head carpenter, James Marshall, was in charge of the work on the south fork of the American River not far from Sutter's Fort, and it was in the tail-race (the water below the wheel) that Marshall made his find:

> I went down as usual, and after shutting off the water from the race I stepped into it, and there upon the rock, about six inches beneath the surface of the water, I DISCOVERED THE GOLD. I was entirely alone at the time . . . .

Sutter swore all his men to secrecy, but it was a secret that simply could not stay kept. Rumours filtered out, and when a shrewd character called Sam Brannan took some gold dust from a talkative miner at Sutter's Fort general store, he realised at once what had happened. It was he who tore down San Francisco's main street, more than 100 kilometres from the strike.

The first rush was purely local, but it was a foretaste, for within a day or two every ship in San Francisco harbour was empty and almost every man and most of the women and children were hitting the trail for Sutter's Fort.

There were only some 14,000 whites in all California at that time, but because those of Spanish descent were not so gold-drunk as Anglo-Americans, only 1,000 or so were involved in the first frantic scramble. This was made more frantic still when lumps weighing more than ten kilos were found.

Meanwhile the news was spreading round the world and ships set out for California, sailing direct from Hawaii and Australia, from Britain and Europe via the gales and high waves of Cape Horn. Americans came from the eastern United States, across the plains and Rockies, or across the fever-ridden swamps and jungles of the Isthmus of Panama, or, like the Europeans, round the Horn. The voyage from New York to San Francisco often took four months or more.

The Horn route was the safest, for the short cut across Panama—there was no canal then—was a killer. The direct way, using the California Trail, should have been reasonably safe as the route was by then so well known, but far too many set out grossly under-equipped for the crossing and fell easy victims to exhaustion, starvation and thirst, and sometimes Indian arrows.

One grim song, *The Fools of Forty-Nine*, summed up the black side of the rush. It mentioned the rotten boats which caused the deaths of some unfortunates, with equally bad food—'With rusty pork and stinking beef and rotten wormy bread.' It mentioned those who were filled with false stories of how easy it was to reach California, how easy to make a fortune. And it finished like this:

> **The people died on every route,**
> **they sickened and died like sheep,**
> **And those at sea before they were dead**
> **were launched into the deep,**
> **And those that died crossing the Plains**
> **fared not as well as that,**
> **For a hole was dug and they was dumped**
> **along the terrible Platte.**

The spring and summer before these horrors had been a wonderful time in California. The goldfields were set in a beautiful area, the weather was perfect, the hunting was good. When the fierce sun of high summer shrank the streams to mere trickles, those first miners saw deposits of gravel with gold in it waiting to be found. One man picked up 1.2 kilograms of gold on his first day in the area. Men panned for gold under a blazing sun as they stood in an ice-cold river for hours at a time. In those first months at least there was a real chance of a man making money, if not his fortune.

Yet few actual miners made real fortunes. Certainly Sutter did not. His lands were invaded by squatters, land which the Supreme Court later stated was not his anyway, and he died poor in 1880, just before Congress finally got around to making amends to him. As for James Marshall, he had an even worse time. The man who had brought untold wealth to California was, indeed, given a small pension for a short time in the 1870s, but he took to drink and it was stopped. He died in 1885.

Some miners made fortunes and even kept them, but the real money-makers were the clever businessmen and traders who supplied the miners with the goods they needed. One Italian, Domenico Ghiradelli, began his rise to millionaire status by selling sweets and chocolates to miners!

The year 1852 was the biggest year of all in the goldfields, for 81 million dollars' worth of gold were extracted, while the population of California had shot up to a quarter of a million, many of them living in booming San Francisco where much of the gold went. By 1900 more than 1,000 million dollars' worth of gold had been found.

By then mining had become highly scientific, and much of it was conducted deep underground. But progress was rapid even in the early days. Soon pick and shovel and the wash pan were

San Francisco was a tiny village in 1848 just before the Gold Rush. By 1851 it looked like this, with a forest of masts in the harbour (Wells Fargo Bank History room)

joined by other tools of the trade. Yet the pan was the father of them all, apart from being useful for frying bacon and washing a shirt in.

Soon miners began to use the cradle, the long tom and the sluice, all of which did the job faster, though they still needed hard work. Later, jets of water ate into hillsides to bring away gold-bearing matter. Yet the pan, for all the exhaustion of using it for hours, was the only method which stopped the tiniest particles from disappearing.

An equal amount of time was given to digging holes and searching for crevices that carried nuggets or flakes. Many nasty accidents occurred on dark nights when people fell down these holes.

But the real victims of the Gold Rush were California's unfortunate Indians, who, unlike the warriors of the Plains, were mostly backward and unwarlike. They were, as far as the tough miners were concerned, 'in the way'. In 1849 there had been some 100,000 Indians—in 1860 only 30,000 were left. The rest had been killed, or decimated by white men's diseases, or by cruel overwork.

The Comstock Lode

By the end of the 1850s, the mining bonanza had spread to other parts of the West, and there at least the Indians gave as good as they got, as many a lonely prospector discovered too late.

Nearly every Western state and territory had its moment of gaudy mining glory, but the greatest strikes of all were in Nevada. There, near the boom town of Virginia City, was the Comstock Lode, always known as the Big Bonanza. Gold was first found there in 1859, but it was the 1873 silver strike which made Virginia City world famous.

The Comstock got its name from a loud-mouthed bully called Henry Comstock, who bluffed two Irishmen out of a gold claim, then sold out before he realised how rich it was. Yet the $16 million or so that the Comstock produced was a mere drop in the ocean compared with what came out of it from 1873 onwards. In 1872, the gold seemed to be played out, but in 1874 it produced $38 million!

The result of the silver-spangled-with-gold strike was that millionaires began to appear all over San Francisco, 300 kilometres west, because much of the money went into property there. Yet there was plenty left in town, as Mark Twain noted:

The classic way to separate gold from earth or gravel was panning. A miner filled his pan with 'dirt', swirled it round under water, then raised it out, still circling it. Every now and then he jerked it in and out of the water to clear the lighter manner. Gold, being heavier than earth, always went to the bottom. (Wells Fargo Bank History Room)

The cradle made life easier, being a wooden box on rockers with a handle to move it. The photo does not show the wooden bars called riffles that kept the gold safe as the miner poured water over the gravel and earth on top of the cradle where there was a strainer (Wells Fargo)

The Californian miners were a mixed bunch, as the photo shows. These are using a sluice, which had riffle bars all the way down to catch the gold (Wells Fargo)

Money was as plenty as dust; every individual considered himself wealthy, and a melancholy countenance was nowhere to be seen. There were military companies, fire companies, brass bands, banks, hotels, theatres, 'hurdy-gurdy houses', wide-open gambling palaces, political pow-wows, civic processions, street fights, murders, inquests, riots, a whisky mill every fifteen steps . . . a dozen breweries and half a dozen jails and station houses in full operation, and some talk of building a church. The 'flush times' were in magnificent flower.

One notable feature of the Comstock story is that the richest men in Virginia City were miners, not traders. One of them, J. P. Jones, counted his dollars by millions and had about five times as many millions as he had fingers and toes!

John Mackay, who reached Virginia City penniless in 1859 with Jack O'Brien, was also destined to strike it rich and become a mining king. As they walked towards the town, O'Brien threw away their last half dollar for luck. 'Let us enter like gentlemen,' he said cheerfully, and in they strolled to fame and fortune.

Mackay deserved every dollar he made. He was a working miner, down one or other of his mines at 6 every day. That, and the use of the most modern engineering methods, brought him success. He lived to see the level of mining go down from one to 450 metres, and he became so expert that he could look at a sample of ore and tell its value more accurately than a professional assayer. He installed the latest machinery and his well-paid men worked regular hours.

Even this greatest single treasure trove in history ran out, but by 1900, when Virginia City had shrunk from 30,000 people to less than 3,000, the Comstock had yielded over half a billion dollars' worth of silver and gold.

A typical Northwestern mining town was Helena, Montana, with its famous Last Chance Gulch (the town's original name). It was a wild spot from the start, being described in 1864 in these words:

Not a day or night passed which did not yield its full fruition of fights, quarrels, wounds, or murders. The crack of the revolver was often heard above the merry notes of the violin . . . Pistols flashed, bowie knives flourished, and oaths filled the air.

Even a short account cannot leave out two wild and woolly mining centres. The first was Deadwood in Dakota Territory, which sprang up after whites had invaded the sacred Black Hills of the

Sioux following an expedition (led by an ambitious young officer named Custer) which had found gold in the hills. In 1876, Custer was to pay for the events he had set in motion when he lost his life at the most famous of all Western battles, 'Custer's Last Stand' at the Little Big Horn.

The second wild town was Tombstone in Arizona, which came into being after a prospector named Ed Schieffelin found a huge silver lode there in 1877. The ferocious Apaches were very much on the warpath, and when Ed told a friend that he was going prospecting for stones (meaning quartz), his friend said: 'The only stone you'll find is your tombstone!' When he named his diggings he remembered this jibe and called them Tombstone.

The Klondike Stampede

In many ways, the last great gold rush was the most rugged of the lot. The Klondike saga belongs to Canadian and American history, though, as usual, men from every part of the world raced to the almost inaccessible spot as soon as the news broke that gold had been found once again.

It was not the first gold strike in Alaska and Canada's Yukon Territory, but it was the first big one. It happened in August 1896 on a tributary of the Klondike River called Rabbit Creek, later renamed Bonanza Creek. George Carmack, an American, and two Indians, Tagish Charley and Skookum Joe, discovered it after the trio had been tipped off by a Canadian named Robert Henderson, who had found a small amount of gold himself. It was a Bonanza indeed, with the gold lying between flaking slabs of rock like the cheese in a huge sandwich.

So far from civilisation was the remote area that at first no one but the local prospectors knew about the find. The first arrivals were the Mounties, a detachment coming complete with Law and Order, almost a novelty in any mining area.

Through the long winter, those who struck it rich gambled and made and lost new fortunes in the small booming village of Dawson, and soon gold was less valuable than salt. Poor Henderson had no part in the joy, for he did not strike it rich. Years later the Canadian Government gave him a pension as part-discoverer of the gold.

Not till July 1897 did news reach the outside world in a most dramatic fashion. Two steamboats packed tight with Bonanza kings reached the ports of Seattle and San Francisco after a long journey down the Yukon and out into the Pacific. Every item of luggage, every jar and every box aboard the ships were crammed full of gold, and as soon as the floating treasure troves docked the world went mad. The name for the new epidemic was Klondicitis and it was very catching.

The world not only went mad: that part of it which set out for the Klondike contained a high percentage of would-be prospectors who were just plain daft. Many had no idea where the Klondike was, or that conditions would vary from rugged to frightful. Some set out overland through British Columbia on a journey which would be tough going even today, others headed northwest via Alberta, still more sailed northwards in mainly overcrowded and often unseaworthy boats and promptly got themselves frozen in for the winter on the Yukon River.

Only one route was worth taking, for many of those who tried the other ways either never got to the Klondike or arrived after the rush was over. The sensible way was to sail to Skagway in Alaska, then cross one of two equally alarming passes, the White and the Chilkoot. After enduring them, the traveller had to sail down the Klondike River at its narrowest and most dangerous, reaching Dawson in home-made craft which could only sail when the ice broke.

Dawson looked like a Wild West town, but was not allowed to behave like one, thanks to Superintendent Sam Steele of the Mounties. He ordered all would-be prospectors to bring in a year's food supply to the Klondike and had the tops of the two passes guarded by his men to see that the rule was obeyed. Without it, there would have been starvation in the goldfields.

A very different man from Steele had Skagway 'sewn up' to such an extent that many Stampeders failed to get clear of the port. He was a criminal named 'Soapy' Smith who seemed very respectable, which helped him in his 'work' of extracting money from people. He had acquired his nickname in Colorado where he managed to 'con' miners that the five-dollar shaving-soap sticks he was offering them might have dollars under their wrappers. The first stick sold would always contain a hundred-dollar bill to inspire confidence. Miners practically got killed in the rush to get at the rest, nearly all of which contained nothing but soap.

Very few prospectors managed to get through Skagway without falling foul of Soapy's unsavoury gang. He controlled everything in Skagway: the Law, the places of entertainment, the carriers who took people's baggage to the top of the passes—at a price. Several journeys were needed to get a year's supplies to the Mounties' posts at the top, so Soapy made a huge profit.

Booming Dawson in 1899, when the Klondike Stampede was at its height. Its storekeepers made more money than most of their customers (Royal Canadian Mounted Police)

Meanwhile Dawson boomed. There were soon more than 40,000 people in town, but not Soapy's gang. The Mounties at the top of the passes saw to it that they never went any further. In 1898, the vast majority of the Stampeders arrived, 30,000 of them sailing down the Yukon in 7,000 home-made boats when the ice broke in the summer. It was a dangerous trip, but when danger loomed at the rapids there was Sam Steele to sort things out.

It was not a long rush. By the spring of 1899 every possible spot had been staked, while the storekeepers made a fortune back in lively but law-abiding Dawson. By 1900 it was over, by which time some £4 million worth of gold had been found in the Klondike. And Dawson began a long decline.

Meanwhile, Skagway had rid itself of Soapy and his gang, urged on by a heroic man named Frank Reid, who killed Soapy but was mortally wounded himself. The gang were not strung up as they well might have been, but either fled or landed in jail. To the credit of the Mounties, in 1898 at the height of the Stampede, there was not a single killing in Dawson.

And the three who started it all? Carmack died rich, Tagish Charley was rich too, but drowned when he was drunk, while Skookum Joe simply went on looking for gold. He was rich as well, but it was the spirit of adventure within him, too, that kept him on the move.

SEEING THE ELEPHANT

'Eureka! Oh how my heart beat! I sat still and looked at it some minutes before I touched it.' So wrote Edward Buffum on finding gold for the first time. He had 'seen the elephant'.

That phrase meant 'seeing gold' in Gold Rush California. The odd origin of the saying is as follows:

There was a farmer who all his life had longed to see an elephant, and at last a circus was coming to town. He filled a wagon with vegetables and eggs and started off, meeting the circus parade on his way. And there leading the parade was an elephant. The farmer was transfixed with joy, but the horses were frightened out of their wits. They began to buck and soon the wagon was overturned and every egg smashed and the vegetables scattered all over the place. As the horses vanished into the distance, the farmer said happily, staring at the great beast: 'I don't give a hang. I have seen the elephant.'

EXIT THE TROOPS

Soldiers were just as eager as sailors to get to the goldfields. From 1 July 1848 to the end of 1849 the Army in northern California lost 716 men out of 1,290. Some were recaptured, but most simply vanished. The men could hardly be blamed. Many were veterans of the war against Mexico and, as local prices soared, their meagre $6 a month was worth just one kilo of flour. Said the acting governor of California: 'The struggle between *right* and six dollars a month and *wrong* and seventy-five dollars a day is rather a severe one.' Most gave up the struggle.

5
THE COWBOYS

The guns fell silent and the long journey home began. Thousands of Texans headed for the Southwest. For four bitter years they had fought for the South in the Civil War and they had lost. Now it was time to rebuild their state, and for many of the returning veterans that meant rebuilding the cattle industry.

Many had to start from the beginning again, for they found their ranches run down or in ruins and thousands of unbranded longhorns running wild.

They set to work at once that summer of 1865, but the task was a tough one. . . .

The American cowboy! Films and television and books have turned him into a legend that has grown with the years, making him seem a romantic figure. Yet his life was·anything but romantic, even if he loved it.

The cowboy's home was the prairie and his roof was the sky. His pay was bad and his food varied from adequate to appalling.

A classic cowboy picture, taken in 1887, Note the binoculars (Library of Congress)

Around four in the morning he got out of his bedroll if he was in the open and stretched himself, and as soon as he could he was on his horse. He lived most of his days in the saddle, and many of his nights, too. It was beneath his dignity to travel far on foot.

His clothes suited his work and his face was tanned with the winds and the sun. He was a working man who could handle himself in any crisis, a man to be depended on.

His story begins in Texas around the 1830s. There had been cowboys further east earlier, and the Spanish had brought long-horn cattle and horses to the Southwest, but it was the American settlers in Texas who made the cattle industry and the Texas cowboy so famous.

The Texans grabbed the cattle they found when they became independent of Mexico in 1836 and developed the Mexican-Texan ranches. Soon the new cattlemen were driving small, then large, herds east to New Orleans, northwards to the settlements of Missouri and, after gold was found, to California. By the time the Civil War started in 1861, Texas was already a cattle kingdom.

It helped that the grass was good in Texas and could survive long periods of drought. The longhorns enjoyed it and that was what mattered. Longhorns! These mean, hard-hided descendants of the first Spanish cattle were nothing like today's highly bred creatures. They were semi-wild and some had horns that spread more than two metres across. A cowboy earned every cent of his miserable forty or so dollars a month looking after them.

The Texas cowboy was a match for the longhorns, though. He had to be, and had to work in every kind of weather, even the terrible winters which could kill thousands of cattle. Most of the cowboys were Americans of British descent, though there were black cowboys and, near the Mexican border, expert *vaqueros*—the Spanish word for cowboys.

Texans did not like Mexicans much, or Indians, townspeople, lawmen, settlers or, especially, sheepherders. Like cowboys all over the West, they said that sheep, which appeared on the ranges in the 1870s, ruined waterholes and cropped grasslands bare. Sometimes cowboys massacred sheep and killed their herders.

Yet if cowboys, especially the Texan variety, were intolerant, they were utterly loyal to their friends and their bosses. They worked hard and would never harm a woman or a child; their courage was total.

Cowboys soon learnt to ride as well as Mexicans or Indians and perform marvels with a rope. They adopted some of the fashions of Mexican *vaqueros*, though they always preferred the stetson hat

A longhorn — mean, moody and magnificent (Denver Public Lib., Western Hist. Dept.)

to the floppy headgear of most *vaqueros*. A stetson made a handy cup, even for a horse. A man could wash in it and it was completely waterproof.

Texans used the Mexican saddle with the big horn to which they tied their rope after lassoing a cow. The leather leg protectors they wore were called chaps (pronounced shaps) from the Spanish word *chaparejos*. Further north woolly chaps were worn. Blue denims were the usual trousers, and the shirt was of wool or cotton, with a waistcoat over it.

A cowboy did not automatically wear a gun. It was usually in his bedroll and sometimes not even in good working order. A pistol and a cartridge belt got in the way of a man working with cattle. When he hit town, though, he wore his shooting-iron, unless a tough cowtown marshal forced him to park it at the bar with the bartender until he left. Cowboys were rarely crack shots with a pistol, though most of them were expert rifle shots.

The big events in a cowboy's life were the spring and autumn roundups and the trail herd north, much of the rest of his time being spent on routine work on the range. He had two headquarters, his bunkhouse where he lived with the other cowhands, and his bedroll, where he not only slept but kept his few belongings on the trail.

The all-important chuck wagon that was his mobile canteen was presided over by a usually cross-tempered Cookie, who would give him a breakfast of perhaps coffee, pancakes and biscuits. Then it was time to work.

He had a string of eight horses assigned to him until he left an outfit, but his saddle was his own property, going wherever he went. He knew how to break in a wild mustang, but the job required such skill that it was often left to experts. Everybody wielded a branding iron to ensure that a rancher's stock was marked. Unbranded animals of unknown origin were called mavericks.

Cowboys rarely sang to their cows at night, for longhorns were so nervy that they would stampede at the slightest sound. Yet another legend, that of the singing cowboy, bites the dust! If a storm was in the air, though, on a dark night, a cowpuncher might hum or sing very softly just to let the cows know he was coming.

Except in town cowboys led a quiet life. Drinking was usually forbidden on a ranch for cowboys needed all their strength for work, and some ranchers even forbade cards because of the quarrels that ensued. Dancing was popular but the shortage of women sometimes led to cowboy dancing with cowboy.

Jobs on the range included looking for strays; mending wire fences when barbed wire, invented in the 1870s, later became

Mixed bathing, cowboy style (Kansas State Historical Society)

widely used; rescuing longhorns from bogs and putting out prairie fires, which could ruin a ranch for years. The lowliest job on the ranch was that of the wrangler, a boy or man in charge of the saddle horses. Heaven help him if his charges fouled or muddied waterholes that the cook wanted to use. Cookie always had a fine line in curses. But *the* job was always the drive north or west up the trail, the most exciting, difficult, dangerous, often maddening, sometimes boring, always grossly underpaid time in a cowboy's life.

Up the Trail

Between 1867 and 1890 cowboys drove ten million longhorns northwards from Texas, saving their state from financial ruin and turning the United States from a nation of pork to beef-eaters. But it had been a long struggle to get the industry going again.

There was not much of a market for cattle in Texas in 1866, but steers were selling at $50 a head, it was said, in the North and East. Not that everyone liked longhorn meat. One paper claimed that it were not fit to eat, but would do to bait traps to catch wolves in. Another said, 'They never eat an ear of corn in their

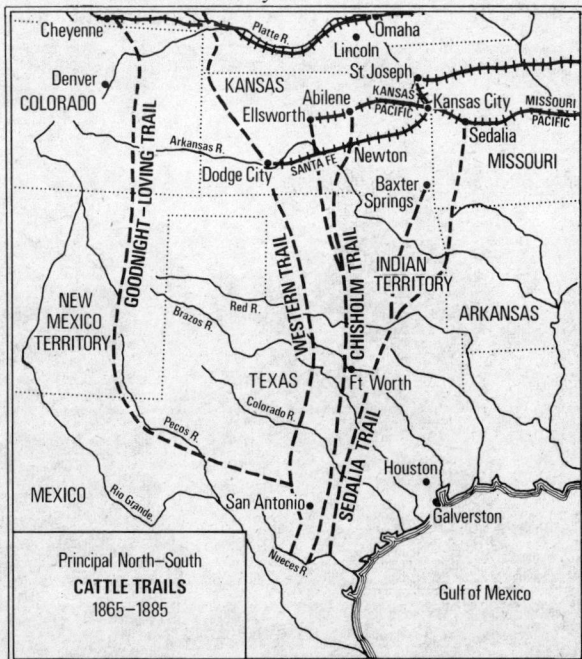

Principal North–South
CATTLE TRAILS
1865–1885

lives . . . Texas cattle are about the nearest thing to wild animals of any now driven to market. We have seen some buffaloes that were more civilized.' That was written in 1854. Would they be more welcome in 1866?

As it happened, the first drive out of Texas after the Civil War was not to Kansas, the state that was above all others to be associated with the cattle drives, but to feed the miners in the mining camps of Colorado over 1,000 kilometres away. The leader was a 30-year-old rancher named Charlie Goodnight, who was to become one of the greatest of all cattle kings.

He teamed up with an older man, Oliver Loving, and, as the Kiowas and Comanches were on the warpath, swung westwards to avoid them before heading north. They had eighteen cowboys and 2,000 longhorns, and hit 130 waterless kilometres almost at the start of their journey. Within three days the cattle were crazed with thirst and when they reached the Pecos River, they plunged in, trampling one another. Many were trapped in quicksands. Finally they reached Colorado.

The cowboys heading north towards eastern Kansas to sell their stock had been less lucky than Goodnight. Everyone seemed anxious to hinder them: rustlers trained in murderous guerilla warfare on the border during the Civil War, Indians who fortu-

Charles Goodnight, the first great cattle king (Western Hist. Collections, U. of Oklahoma Lib.)

nately only wanted token payment for the right to cross their lands, and farmers who resented the fact that longhorns carried tick fever north which killed Kansas cattle, though longhorns were immune. Quarantine laws banned Texas cattle from most parts of Kansas for much of the year, which backed up the farmers' objections legally. The situation was grim.

Salvation came in 1867 in the shape of a cattle dealer called Joseph McCoy from Illinois. He knew the Texans' problems, decided that a trail must be blazed west of the anti-cowboy settlements, and daringly decided to make Chicago, in his home state of Illinois far to the Northeast, not St. Louis, Missouri, the headquarters of the cattle business. But he needed a point from which to ship the longhorns north.

Railroads were already crossing Kansas and he searched for many weeks to find the right place, finally choosing the tiny Kansas hamlet of Abilene on the railroad. It had a few huts and a single street, whose chief attraction was a prairie dog colony in the middle of it, but there was good grass nearby and water. He rapidly had pens built and a siding for cattle trucks, meanwhile sending messages deep into Texas telling Texans to drive their longhorns to Abilene.

Jessie Chisholm, who blazed the great trail that bears his name (Oklahoma Hist. Soc.)

A trail already existed, blazed by a half-Cherokee Indian, half-Scottish trader called Jesse Chisholm, and it was the Chisholm Trail that the cowboys used, driving a few thousand cattle up it in 1867 and an amazing 600,000 by 1871. The men were on the trail for up to four months.

The Chisholm and other trails were run as strictly as military operations, for discipline was vital. The trail boss rode in front, not too fast, for the cattle needed their fair share of grass or they would arrive underweight at the cowtown. So he aimed at sixteen to twenty kilometres a day. On each side of the leading longhorns was a point rider, then swing men and flank men and, finally, the unfortunate drag men bringing up the rear and eating dust all day. The drag men had to stop stragglers and attend to weaklings, and as the job was so unpleasant cowboys normally took it in turn. The wrangler with the horses rode to one side of the column, while Cookie in his chuck wagon was also on the side, near the front. He carried bedrolls as well as molasses, beans, cornmeal etc. And there was always beef 'on the hoof' to be had for dinner.

Apart from obvious human perils from outlaws and Indians, there were several dangerous natural ones. Prairie storms, especially hailstorms, could be lethal. Lightning on the Plains could be very frightening, while some hailstones were big enough to kill a cow or knock a cowboy out cold.

Every river crossing was dangerous, even if the trail boss had found firm banks and a spot where the stream was shallow enough for an easy crossing. The cowboys had to keep the cattle moving, for a holdup could turn into a water stampede. Sometimes a piece of floating driftwood hitting the leading longhorn could start a stampede. No wonder it often took several days to cross some rivers. And if the river beds seemed dry there were often quicksands which swallowed up the leading cows.

There was nothing to equal the danger of a land stampede, which could even be started by the scent of distant water. When a stampede started the cowboys had to get the cattle into a great circle and slow them down, which might take days. Many cattle could be killed in a stampede, and many a cowboy was buried on the 'lone prairie' after being trampled to death by thousands of thundering feet. Outlaws and Indians both deliberately started stampedes, and even cowboys had to sometimes, usually if they knew that poisonous water lay directly ahead.

The Cowtowns

The longhorns were coming!

To those watching them approaching the cowtown they seemed like a moving duststorm out of which riders advanced to hire shipping pens and find buyers. Another herd had reached the railhead.

What were these cowtowns of the 1860s and 70s like—Abilene, Newton, Wichita, Dodge City and the rest? Most of them had a railroad running through the centre, with the respectable folk living on the 'right side of the tracks', while on the 'wrong' side were the saloons and gambling joints and dance halls waiting to entertain a Texas cowboy after he had hit town. There he had a bath, the first, possibly, in a thousand kilometres, burnt his old, vermin-ridden clothes—you couldn't keep clean on the trail—and bought himself a new suit.

Townspeople had very mixed feelings about the Texans. They made a living from them, but they were also frightened of them. One Kansas reporter wrote about them as follows:

His diet is principally Navy plug and whisky, and the occupation of his heart is gambling. . . . He generally wears a revolver

Front Street, Dodge City, Kansas, 1878 (Western Hist. Collections, U. of Oklahoma Lib.)

on each side, which he will use with as little hesitation on a man as on a wild animal. Such a character is dangerous and desperate, and each had generally killed his man. There are good and even honorable men among them, but run-away boys and men who find it too hot for them even in Texas join the cattle drovers and constitute a large proportion of them. They drink, swear, and fight; and life with them is a round of boisterous gaiety. . . .

After weeks on the trail they were bound to go wild. In Newton's single year as a cowtown the sound of gunfire was non-stop from dawn till midnight, while at Abilene rampaging Texans set fire to saloons when drunk on rot-gut booze, and when sober they were also destroyers of property. When the citizens of Abilene erected a jail, the Texans tore it apart, then tore down its replacement. They also liked riding into saloons. When leaving town the Texans peppered every building in sight. The only surprising thing was how few people were actually killed. Not that drunks were accurate shots, and folk learned to keep their heads down. Only on Texas Street, where the main places of entertainment were, was there always a welcome.

But even in the wildest days there were always a few quiet saloons where a man could talk business, listen to music and enjoy good wine, worlds away from the whisky the boys were drinking, so strong and coarse that it was said it would make a rabbit fight a bulldog!

The Cattle Kings

The cowboy would hit the trail for home, probably after having blown all his money in one gigantic spree. He returned to the ranch or went his way elsewhere. Money meant little to him. He left that to the cattle kings.

Some of these bosses of the cow country were ex-cowboys, but all were businessmen out to make money. They were not all American. There were British, French and German ranchers on the range, and many ranches were run from a distance by British money. The big ranchers really believed they were kings, while their wives were the queens of the prairies. Yet all were hospitable. It was a rule of the range that no man was turned away hungry from a ranch.

Cattle kings rarely bothered with guns, leaving that to their men. Only a man with a death wish would try and kill one of them, for his cowhands had a habit of killing those who 'annoyed'

John Chisum, a Southwestern cattle king (Western History Collections, U. of Oklahoma Library)

the boss. Some ranchers were good to their men, some were not, some were never there, leaving managers in charge. All were men to be reckoned with.

In the early days, from 1867 onwards, the Chisholm and later trails were crowded with cattle heading for the gaudy cowtowns of Kansas, and until the 1880s the trail herds continued. By then barbed wire, extensively used, but at first bitterly resented by cattlemen, had come to stay. So the old open-range system with cattle wandering freely came to an end. Besides, by now there were thousands of cattle living on the northern plains. Settlers, too, arrived in the cattleman's West in increasing numbers in the 70s and 80s, which often led to bitter range wars, but in the end cowboys and farmers (also referred to as 'sodbusters', 'squatters' and 'nesters') learned to live together.

The worst disaster that hit the range was a natural one. The winters of 1886 and 1887 nearly destroyed the cattle industry. At least half of all the cows on the range died, possibly as many as 80 per cent, and to add to the woes of the ranchers the price of beef fell. But those who survived became more efficient, concentrating on better breeds of cattle from Britain, including white-faced Herefords, which had already begun to replace longhorns. They developed new breeds, and generally adopted a more efficient and scientific approach to ranching. Now they no longer had any objection to barbed wire, and just a few began looking at sheep with interest instead of hatred. Times were changing.

Did cowboys ever go on strike?

The hands of three Texas ranches did in 1883 to try to get their wages up from thirty dollars a month to fifty. Soon two hundred cowpunchers were out, but, alas, they whooped it up in the town of Tascosa instead of attending the business of running a strike, and soon the ranchers were taking on drifting cowhands at the usual rate. The strikers returned to work at thirty dollars a month or left the range altogether.

How did the cowboy get his name?

Strangely enough, nobody knows for certain. During the American Revolution (1775-83), when Britain's American colonies gained their independence, local guerilla fighters who supported the British, and who helped themselves to cattle, became known as 'cowboys', and for many years the term was used almost as an insult. In Texas those herding cattle were known in the early days as 'drovers', and the men who drove the first herds up the trail to Kansas were known by that name until the early 1870s, when the more familiar 'cowboy' became common.

How tough were cowboys?

Cowboys were tough, but not as tough as they liked to pretend: no one could be. Photographers encouraged them to look suitably 'mean', even supplying them with dummy guns if they had not 'brought their own.'

A typical tough cowpoke story concerns an Indian chief and General Phil ('the only good Indian is a dead one') Sheridan:

Chief: 'Gimme cannon.'

Sheridan: 'What! Do you want to kill my soldiers with it?'

Chief: 'No. Want to kill cowboy. Kill soldier with a club.'

Isom Dart, black cowboy (Denver Public Library, Western Hist. Dept.)

Injured cowboy being treated by his friends (Kansas State Hist. Soc.)

A ranch in Crook County, Wyoming (Wyoming State Archives & Hist. Dept.)

The Marquis de Morès, a Frenchman who became a cattle king in Dakota Territory (State Historical Society of N. Dakota)

6
FRONTIER JUSTICE

When Wild Bill Hickok, the 'Prince of Pistoleers', was shot in the back of the head by Jack McCall, the *Black Hills Pioneer* reported the event formally:

> Died, in Deadwood, Black Hills, August 2, 1876, from the effect of a pistol shot, J. B. Hickok, (Wild Bill) formerly of Cheyenne, Wyoming. Funeral Services will be held in Charlie Utter's camp, on Thursday afternoon, August 3, 1876, at 3 o'clock. All are respectfully invited to attend.

The Wild West had claimed one of its most distinguished victims.

When the Civil War ended in 1865, thousands of ex-soldiers headed West along with settlers, outlaws, miners, killers and gamblers. Many cowboys decided to live outside the Law and make an easier living, in fact most of the famous outlaws, except the James brothers, were cowpunchers at some time in their careers. It was high time for Law and Order to go West as well, for the army could only be called in if the government decided a state of near war existed.

Frontier justice was rough, especially in pre-Civil-War California's gold rush days. The miners themselves cleaned up the goldfields of 1849 by arranging instant 'necktie parties' for villains caught in the act, and some who were innocent, but presumed guilty, were hung. Then it was San Francisco's turn.

By 1850 the fast-growing city was a paradise for thieves and murderers. After early gangs of terrorists had been banished by a rising of townspeople against them, a new bunch of ruffians called the Sydney Ducks, or Coves, turned night-time San Francisco into a terrifying place. So great were the crimes of these mainly British ex-convicts from Australia that two hundred citizens formed the first Vigilance Committee to stamp them out. They rallied at the sound of a bell and swiftly tried and hanged a thief called Jenkins to the cheers of the populace, the annoyance of the official police and the alarm of the Ducks. After a few more hangings and some mass banishments, the Vigilantes, having done what they had set themselves up to do, disbanded.

They went to work again in 1855, this time to stamp out local villains whom the corrupt city government would not deal with. After hanging several killers, they again disbanded.

Wild Bill Hickok, the Prince of Pistoleers, in buckskins in the 1860s. Later he often dressed in the height of fashion (Kansas State Historical Society)

The Vigilante system spread rapidly. Some Vigilantes were nothing more than masked lynch mobs, but many carried on the San Francisco tradition and ran themselves as an organised body of dedicated men.

In Montana in 1864 the gold-mining area was being terrorised by an emperor of crime named Henry Plummer. Not that anyone suspected him at first. Despite a notorious career of violence and robbery in other parts of the West, he looked a man to be trusted at all times. His manners were perfect, he radiated decency and honesty.

Plummer's final triumph was to get himself elected as Sheriff of Bannack when he was unofficially running a one-hundred-strong gang of highwaymen, known locally as road agents. These unsavoury characters had one object in life, to part miners and travellers from their belongings, violently if necessary.

The handsome, so plausible, Plummer had a number of lodging houses near the mines which were all staffed by his fellow criminals. Every stagecoach worth robbing was marked by them, and his boys all wore special knots in their ties to identify each other. They christened themselves 'The Innocents'!

Plummer's Reign of Terror was threatened when some citizens at last began to suspect him, and formed vigilance committees. But only when an Innocent confessed were they able to take action. Plummer, too vain by this time to realise his danger, was caught and strung up, and so were other Innocents. The Vigilantes soon broke up the rest of the gang.

Even the tough Vigilantes of Montana could hardly have coped with the nightmare that was Kansas and Missouri before the Civil War. There, murderous pro-slavery gangs and equally murderous anti-slavery gangs killed each other and anyone who got in their way.

During the Civil War murderers trained in these Border Wars of Kansas became barbarous guerilla fighters. They included the notorious Jesse and Frank James and their kinsmen, the Youngers. Incredibly, Jesse was to become America's Robin Hood, though he never robbed the rich to pay the poor. But as his hobby was robbing Northern banks, plenty of Southern folk, so recently defeated by the North, supported the supposedly misunderstood young man. One of his own men, Bob Ford, finally killed him in 1882, being unable to resist the bounty money offered by railroads which had been regularly robbed by the James boys in the 1870s.

They put a white shaft beside his grave later, with an inscription:

The Hangman's Tree in Helena, Montana, a mining town where the miners took the law into their own hands (Montana Historical Society)

Jesse W. James,
Died April 3, 1882
Aged 34 years, six months, 28 days.
Murdered by a coward whose name is
not worthy to appear here.

Bob Ford was blasted to death with a shotgun eleven years later, after accusing a man named Kelly of stealing a diamond ring.

Films, television, books and legends have made everyone believe in a mythical 'Code of the West' where men faced each other at high noon on dusty streets and obeyed set rules of duelling. In fact, many Frontier killings were sheer murder (like Hickok's death at the hands of McCall) and many so-called gunfights were sordid affairs in back streets at close range. Some were just drunken brawls.

There were some, though, that matched the film version. In Springfield, Missouri, one day in 1865, Wild Bill Hickok fought Dave Tutt after a quarrel over a woman and cards. The fight took place on the town square and there were plenty of onlookers. The range was 68 metres and Tutt, ignoring Wild Bill's warning not to cross the square, advanced, drawing his pistol. Wild Bill drew one of his two Colt Navy revolvers, shot Tutt through the heart as the latter's bullet sped harmlessly by him, then wheeled round on Tutt's friends.

'Aren't you satisfied, gentlemen?' he asked. 'Put up your shootin' irons, or there'll be more dead men here.'

Men like Hickok had nerves of steel. Top gunslingers usually shot first and asked questions afterwards and they tended not to risk shoot-outs with other experts.

Quick on the Draw

Every filmgoer imagines that famous gunslingers had quick-as-lightning draws, and some certainly did, though not as swift as modern experts with equally modern holsters and pistols. But the modern fast guns are just playing games. They do not have to face up to a killer like John Wesley Hardin, cold-eyed and bent on killing.

What mattered was accuracy and that meant taking one's time, though drawing from holsters on the hip or the shoulder, or from the pocket or belt was better done fast than slowly. And many gunslingers already had their pistols drawn on their way to a fight. If there was a Code of the West it was this: shoot an unarmed man and it ranks as murder; but if he is armed, even if he is facing the other way, you should get acquitted at the trial. Of course you may get lynched later by the dead man's pals.

Henry Plummer was no slouch with a six-gun. Thomas Dimsdale, who wrote the classic *The Vigilantes of Montana,* recalled:

The headquarters of the marauders was Rattlesnake Ranch . . . Two rods [ten metres] in front of this building was a sign post, at which they used to practice with their revolvers. They were capital shots. Plummer was the quickest hand with his revolver of any man in the mountains. He could draw the pistol and discharge the five loads in three seconds. The post was riddled with holes, and was looked upon as quite a curiosity until it was cut down. . . .

A lighthearted account of six-shooting prowess was written by Mark Twain, a Westerner in his early days. The date is 1861:

Slade was a matchless marksman with a navy revolver. The legends say that one morning at Rocky Ridge, when he was feeling comfortable, he saw a man approaching who had offended him some days before—observe the fine memory he had for matters like that—and, 'Gentlemen,' said Slade, drawing, 'it is a good twenty-yard shot—I'll clip the third button on his coat!' Which he did. The bystanders all admired it. And they all attended the funeral too.

Some gunfighters wore two guns, but rarely fired both at once, except in a saloon brawl, or as a defence against a mass of attackers. The second gun was a reserve for an emergency or when the first was empty. The main reason it had come into use in the first place was that the early revolvers, before the invention of metallic cartridges like today's, took longer to load and were liable to jam, which made an extra gun a necessity. Once there were enough metallic cartridges, the second gun disappeared. Besides few top gunslingers were equally good shots with both hands.

It was in the cowtowns that many of the classic confrontations between law and disorder took place. The Law usually consisted of a marshal, an assistant and a number of policemen who might or might not be good men in a tight spot. Abilene, as we have seen, literally had no law at all when the first Texans came to town. They took particular delight in shooting up posters which suggested that firearms should not be carried within the city limits. But in 1870 the situation changed dramatically.

T. C. Henry, the mayor, hired a tall, good-looking marshal

named Tom Smith after a succession of lawmen had proved incapable of maintaining law and order. He took the job, with the proviso that pistols would have to be banned. 'As well contend with a frenzied maniac as an armed and drunken cowboy,' he told Henry. Then he went out on his first patrol, wearing his six-guns, and on this very first patrol a cowboy named Big Hank sauntered up to him, having heard of his arrival.

'Are you the man who thinks he's gonna run this town?' enquired Big Hank with a leer.

'I'll trouble you to hand me your pistol now,' retorted Smith. He was always polite.

Big Hank swore and Tom Smith asked once more, then felled him with his sledgehammer fists. He took Hank's gun and told him to get out of town. Hank went.

News of this feat, which shook the Texans, who were used to guns not fists, spread far and wide in the cow camps. The next day Wyoming Frank rode in to challenge the new marshal. He was soon drunk and began boasting what he would do to the lawman.

Down the street came Tom Smith and asked Wyoming Frank for his gun, keeping too close to him to allow him to draw. Wyoming Frank found himself backed into a saloon where, in front of a tense crowd, the dialogue of the previous day was

Tom Smith, Marshal of wild and woolly Abilene in 1870 (Kansas State Hist. Soc.)

repeated—and the knock-out blow.

'I'll give you five minutes to get out of town,' said Smith. 'And don't you ever again let me set eyes on you.'

The owner of the saloon came round his counter and said to the marshal: 'That was the nerviest act I ever saw. You did your duty and the coward got what he deserved. Here's my gun. I reckon I'll not need it as long as you're marshal of this town.'

Others came forward with their pistols and Smith told them to leave them with the barman till they went back to their camps. This was the beginning of the famous cowtown edict: 'Park your shootin' irons at the bar.'

All that summer, the busiest in Abilene's history, not one man was killed on its streets. Tom Smith rode down them dominating the scene but never using his guns, only his fists when he had to. Tragically, though, after the cattle season was over, he was murdered, not by cowboys, but by two settlers beyond the town limits.

The following summer a different type of town-tamer was hired—Wild Bill Hickok, who rarely used his fists. Already cursed by a reputation as a top gunslinger, he was forced to use his pistols to survive and took every precaution. He avoided bright lights and dark alleyways, and he got through the season alive. But an innocent man was killed in a fight. Hickok had an argument—to

Wyatt Earp, head of a notorious clan of brothers.
(Kansas State Hist. Soc.)

65

put it mildly—with a gambler named Phil Coe, who was supported by some fifty Texans, most of them armed. Coe was
mortally wounded by Wild Bill in a sudden duel at only eight
paces, but at that moment another man came dashing through the
darkness, pistol in hand, and was killed in the crossfire. It was Mike
Williams, Hickok's friend.

That was almost the last incident in Abilene's history as a
cowtown, for the citizens decided to tell the cowboys to head
elsewhere in 1872. Hickok and Abilene parted company. For a few
lively years the action switched to other towns like Wichita,
Ellsworth and Newton, and the 'Queen of the Prairies', Dodge City.

Wyatt Earp was an assistant marshal in Dodge for a time, and
his friend Bat Masterson served there too, later dying with his
boots off as a New York sports reporter. Yet another Dodge peace
officer, Bill Tilghman, was more like the film and story-book
marshal than any of the other lawmen. He became a legendary
figure in Oklahoma, where even his enemies liked him. The
notable bad man, Bill Doolin, once told his men not to murder
Bill. 'He's too good a man to be shot in the back,' said Doolin. It
looked as if the marshal would die in bed, but when he was
seventy, he was shot down by a drunken official. He got his stated
wish and died with his boots on.

Gunfight at the O.K. Corral

Wyatt Earp managed to die with his off in 1929 when he was
eighty years old. They are still arguing about him in the West,
some claiming him as a knight in shining armour, others as a
corrupt lawman and vicious killer. The truth? Somewhere in
between no doubt. His most famous exploit was the 'Gunfight at
the O.K. Corral' in Tombstone, Arizona, in 1881. He walked there
with his six-shooter in his hand under his coat, and with him
walked two of his brothers and also his dentist-gunfighter friend,
Doc Holliday, to do battle with the five-strong Clanton gang.
Films about the famous fight carefully avoid the fact that it all
took place in a single, bullet-laden minute, the rather shady
lawmen and their very shady friend beating their cattle-rustling
opponents in a haze of gunsmoke. Morgan Earp had a bullet in
his shoulder and Virgil Earp one in his leg, while two of their
opponents were dead, one was dying and two more were running
away.

The sheer size of the West made it difficult, sometimes impossible, to keep crime at bay, and there were not always Vigilantes

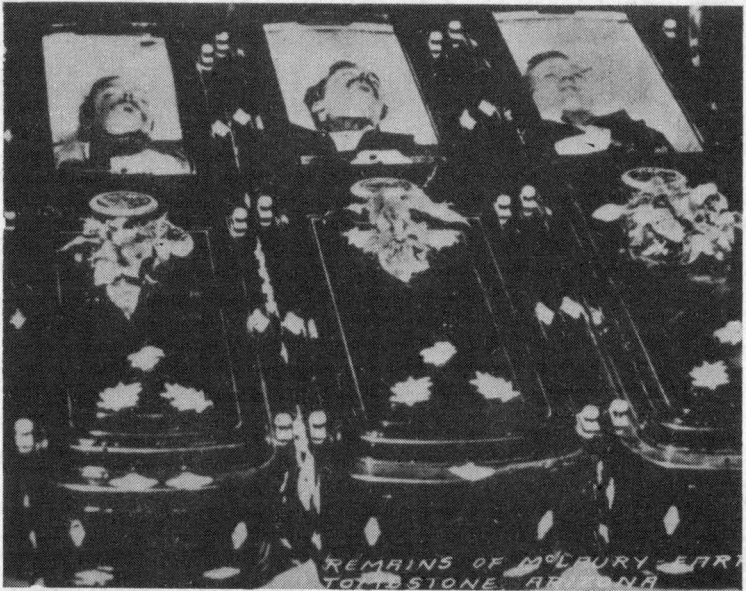

Slain at the O.K. Corral (Arizona Historical Society)

(good or bad) to arrange necktie parties. One Nevada mining camp was 480 kilometres from the nearest sheriff. Few jails could stand up to a really well-organised and powerful rescue attempt. The only reasonably safe prisons were the territorial or state ones.

In Texas, a handful of tough Texas Rangers helped tame a huge, wild area between the 1840s and 1890s. They were helped at the start by being the first to use Samuel Colt's five-shot revolvers—six-shooters came later—which gave them a huge advantage over Indians and outlaws until they, too, got rapid-firing weapons.

Billy the Kid

The Law rarely managed to stop range wars and bitter feuds, and certainly contributed little at first to the epic Lincoln County War. Billy the Kid was the star performer in that murderous conflict. Born around 1859, probably in New York, and called Henry McCarty, he is better known as William Bonney, but is best known as Billy the Kid or simply the Kid.

After various adventures, he took a job as a cowhand on a ranch in Lincoln County, New Mexico, run by a young Englishman named John Tunstall, who took a liking to the youth and

Billy the Kid — Robin Hood or Frontier Hoodlum, misunderstood young man or trigger-happy murderer? His story remains fascinating (National Archives)

encouraged him. Tunstall and his lawyer-storekeeper friend, Alexander McSween, had fallen out with an ambitious rancher and politician called Major Murphy. Tunstall was backed by cattle king John Chisum, Murphy by political friends, including the territorial governor. Both sides had plenty of supporters and the result was—gunsmoke!

First the Murphy gang gunned down Tunstall in cold blood. They say that Billy swore a great oath over his body, vowing to kill the murderers. He got off to a good start as one of a band who shot down a Murphy man, Sheriff Brady, and his deputy, on the streets of Lincoln. The next encounter was less successful.

A posse of Tunstall-McSween men were held off at a spot called Blazer's Mill by a leathery character called 'Buckshot Andrew' Roberts, so named for buckshot in one of his shoulders. He killed the Kid's friend Dick Brewer and wounded two more before dying from lead poisoning.

The full story of what happened next cannot be given here: it would take the rest of the book! But there were highlights. A five-day battle raged in the streets of Lincoln with the Murphy gang besieging the McSween store, one of the defenders being Billy. The climax came when the store was set on fire. The women ran out unharmed, then Billy and the men exited, six-guns belching. McSween fell dead and so did three more, but Billy escaped.

There was a warrant out for him for the slaying of Sheriff Brady, so at first he laid low, occasionally stealing horses and cattle. The Kid was soon 'King of the Outlaws' leading his own picked bunch of desperadoes. One of the reasons he stayed free was that most Mexicans and many Americans liked him. But one of his friends turned enemy, a tall, determined man in need of a job. His name was Pat Garrett. He became sheriff of Lincoln County and, knowing Billy's hide-outs, finally brought him to justice. Or so he thought.

Billy was tried for the murder of Sheriff Brady, though he was only one of the killers, and no one else on either side was ever tried for their part in the War. He was sent to the Murphy store in Lincoln, now turned into a jail, to await hanging. Two deputies guarded him night and day.

They both died at the Kid's hands, so the actual way that Billy escaped is still argued about. The most probable version is as follows:

He was manacled hand and foot and watched continually by Deputies Olinger and Bell, but his friends managed to smuggle a pistol into the washroom. One night, Olinger went across the road to have his supper. At once Billy asked to visit the washroom and clanked his way there. A minute later he returned with the gun and ordered Bell into a side room. The deputy made a run for it and got a bullet in the back which sent him crashing down the stairs dead. Billy hobbled to the armoury, grabbed Olinger's loaded shotgun and went to a second-floor window to see the other deputy hurrying back from his meal, alerted by the shots.

'Hullo, Bob,' called Billy and blasted Olinger full of buckshot. Then he ordered the janitor to bring him a file and a horse. He had already escaped from his handcuffs, having discovered that his small, thin hands could slip out of the heavy regulation-issue cuffs. Moments later he was riding away with a grin on his face.

Where was Pat Garrett that night? Away from town ordering the gallows for Billy's hanging!

Furiously Pat Garrett went back to work and finally tracked Billy down to Fort Sumner. There are several versions of the Kid's death in 1881 at the hand of his old friend, who himself was shot and killed in 1908. Garrett's grave has no monument, but Billy's has been a major tourist attraction ever since.

Roy Bean was an appalling judge, but a great character. He loved the Jersey-born actress, Lily Langtry, from afar, even if her name was spelt incorrectly (National Archives)

Judge Roy Bean

Few judges made much of a mark in such violent times, though two were famous. Judge Roy Bean was a self-taught comedian who was 'the Law west of the Pecos'. He ran a saloon-cum-courtroom known as The Jersey Lilly in honour of the British actress, Lily Langtry—he mis-spelt Lily—who had been born in Jersey and whom he worshipped from afar. His judgements were off-beat. When an Irishman killed a Chinaman he ruled: 'Gentlemen, the court finds that the law is explicit on the killing of a fellow man, but nothing at all is said about knocking off a Chinaman. Case dismissed.'

'Hanging Judge' Parker

'Hanging Judge' Parker was no comedian, but a stern dispenser of justice at Fort Smith, Arkansas, which was on the edge of Indian Territory (later Oklahoma) and a hide-out for many desperate men. (Those who saw the John Wayne film, *True Grit*, will have some idea what things were like in Parker's day.) Mass hangings of six a time on a gallows built for twelve were a speciality of Judge Parker's.

Also helping tame the West were Pinkerton's detectives. 'I rode 100 miles today,' wrote the founder's son Robert Pinkerton. 'I am determined that these men must be placed behind bars.' They had a 'rogues' gallery' of photographs on file, plus details of wanted men. They led the hunt against the Renos, who staged the first train robbery in 1866, they acted against the James gang and against Butch Cassidy and the Wild Bunch, and they helped put many a man behind bars or under the ground.

Alan Pinkerton, founder of the famous detective agency
(Pinkerton's National Detective Agency Inc.)

'Bloody Bill' Anderson, a Southern guerilla leader who terrorised mid-Western states in the Civil War. His gang included Jesse and Frank James and the Youngers (State Hist. Soc. of Missouri)

Sheriff Commodore Perry Owens marched up to a house in Holbrook, Arizona, in 1887 to bring in a horse thief and took on a whole family of killers. He killed three, wounded a fourth, and walked away unharmed (Arizona Historical Society)

War in Wyoming

One of the last major outbreaks of lawlessness in the West was the Johnson County War in Wyoming. In 1890 the ranchers of Wyoming were fighting mad with the homesteaders and squatters on the range, regarding them as nothing better than rustlers. Some of them may have been, but most were simply honest settlers trying to make a living for themselves and their families.

The first signs of 'war' came when 'Cattle Kate' Watson and a friend of hers named Averill, whose store was said to be a hide-out for local rustlers, were hanged. Averill had dared to contest the decision of the Wyoming Stock Growers' Association that all unbranded calves should be branded with the Association's special mark.

The homesteaders of Johnson County elected Red Angus, sympathetic to their cause, as sheriff, while detectives employed by the Association prepared a list of seventy alleged rustlers. Some no doubt were cattle thieves, others were settlers who happened to be 'in the way', using land that could be restored to cattle.

The Association formed a vigilance committee called the Regulators and hired some Texas gunslingers who, along with equally trigger-happy local gunfighters, made up a fifty-two-strong army that proceeded to invade Wyoming in April 1892. A Major Frank Woolcott, and an unsavoury, cold-eyed Texan gunfighter named Frank Canton, led the 'army', which had some newspapermen with it. The reporters, fed with propaganda, imagined that the gallant fifty-two were going to stamp out a gang of vicious killers and robbers.

They chose a bad first target, the K.C. Ranch, which was owned by Nate Champion. The invaders had hoped to isolate their enemies by cutting all the telegraph wires in Johnson County. They expected to deal smartly with Champion then move on to the next name on the list. Champion had other ideas. He had a friend with him, Nick Rae, but Rae was wounded when he stepped out of Nate's hut firing at his enemies and Nate dragged him dying inside. Nate kept up a day-long battle and even found time to keep a diary of events.

During the day a neighbour passed the siege and sped to the town of Buffalo, which was the settlers' headquarters, raising the alarm. But luck had run out for the heroic Nate Champion. His assailants decided to set fire to his house by rolling a wagon load of burning straw down on to it. He dashed out, rifle and pistol in his hands, to die under a hail of bullets.

In his pocket was found his siege diary which ended with these words:

> Shooting again. I think they will fire the house this time. It's not night yet. The house is all fired. Goodbye, boys, if I never see you again. NATHAN D. CHAMPION.

His killers put a label on his body CATTLE THIEVES—BEWARE! though even his enemies admired him. Meanwhile the settlers, led by Red Angus the sheriff, were thoroughly roused and the K.C. Ranch's besiegers were to find themselves under siege. But the then President of the United States, under the false impression that Johnson County's settlers were in a state of open rebellion, sent in the cavalry to deal with the situation. The soldiers 'rescued' the invaders, who felt suitably sheepish, then lawyers took over. So great was the influence of the cattle kings that the hired killers got off scot free and the cattlemen claimed a victory. But they and everyone else knew who had really won. The settlers were there to stay and the ranchers had to learn to get along with them.

Who was John Wesley Hardin?
John Wesley Hardin, the preacher's son, became perhaps the most deadly of them all. Without remorse, he admitted to killing at least forty-four men. Born in 1853, he grew up when Texas was in turmoil just after the Civil War, but his evil temper was more to blame than the times in which he lived. He was caught by the Texas Rangers in 1878 and sentenced to twenty-five years in prison, and there he studied law. Paroled in 1894, he tried to settle down, but was shot in the back of the head by John Selman. His exciting *Life of John Wesley Hardin,* which ends at the point when he decided to study law in prison, is regarded as genuine, if not always entirely accurate. It has been republished by the University of Oklahoma Press.

Did any badmen remotely resemble Robin Hood?
Not really. The nearest was a not-very-successful outlaw called Sam Bass, who had a passion for horse-racing and got bored with being a cowboy. He and his gang pulled off one major train robbery and he did give money away in a friendly fashion before the Texas Rangers caught up with him, killing him in 1878.

When did the badmen's Wild West really end?
Around the beginning of this century. When Butch Cassidy and

The Wild Bunch. Front l to r: Harry Longbaugh (the Sundance Kid), Ben Kilpatrick, Butch Cassidy. Back l to r: Bill Carver, Harvey Logan
(Pinkerton's Detective Agency)

The posse formed to combat the Wild Bunch going aboard their specially converted train
(Union Pacific Railroad)

Calamity Jane, plainswoman and teller of tall tales, even claiming that she and Wild Bill Hickok were married (National Archives)

REWARD

WELLS, FARGO & CO.'S EXPRESS BOX

on COAST LINE STAGE CO'S ROUTE, from Soledad, was ROBBED this morning, by two men, about ten miles north of San Miguel.

$250 Each

will be paid for ARREST and CONVICTION of the Robbers.

JNO. J. VALENTINE, Gen. Supt.

San Francisco, July 15, 1875.

Reward poster (Wells Fargo Bank History Room)

A wells Fargo chest (Wells Fargo Bank History Room)

Belle Starr was a tough character who preferred cattle rustling to cooking. Here she is with a half-Indian friend named Blue Duck. Sometime before she was killed she said: 'I regard myself as a woman who has seen much of life' (Oklahoma Hist. Soc.)

the Sundance Kid headed for South America in 1902 it was a sign that times were changing. One of their associates in the Wild Bunch, Ben Kilpatrick, alias the Tall Texan, tried a train hold-up as late as 1912 and got killed for his pains. Butch (born Robert LeRoy Parker) and the Sundance Kid (Harry Longbaugh) are thought to have perished under a hail of bullets in Bolivia (as they did in the famous film), but there are many who believe the story put about by Butch's sister that he and his friend returned to live and die peacefully in the West, and that another pair of 'Yanquis' died; there were quite a few by then in South America.

What were the most popular weapons in the West?
The Colt New Model Army of 1873, which was the 'Peacemaker,' and the equally famous Winchester rifle, model of 1873. Samuel Colt's revolvers, which were to allow even a skinny weakling to stand up to a man mountain if the weakling had practised long and hard, were first in action in the 1830s and 40s against the Seminole Indians of Florida, then used to deadly effect by the Texas Rangers against the Comanches.

The early Colt revolvers were 'percussion', which meant that they were loaded with powder and ball, the charge being set off by a copper cap filled with fulminate of mercury. The 'Peace-maker' had 'fixed' or metallic ammunition, cap, powder and ball being contained in a brass or copper case.

Were Belle Starr and Calamity Jane as tough as they made out?
Belle was extremely tough; Calamity liked to pretend that she was and had a genius for telling tall stories, including ones about her alleged romance with Wild Bill Hickok. A tougher character by far was Suffolk-born 'Poker Alice' Tubbs, a noted lady gambler, whose motto was: 'I never run a crooked game and never gamble on a Sunday.' One weekday drunken soldiers burst into her club and she shot one dead. 'I cannot find it in my heart to send a white-haired old lady to prison,' said the judge, and let her go free.

7
TRAVEL—WESTERN STYLE

Steamboats

'The devil is coming, blowing fire and smoke out of his nose and kicking the water back with his feet.'

That is what the Indians are alleged to have shouted when they saw a steamboat coming up the Colorado River against the current, but they got used to the devil and supplied the steamboat owners with wood to burn.

Steamboats reached the West before either railroads or stagecoaches. Some of them were floating palaces complete with every luxury that their owner-captains could afford. Others were more like armoured gunboats ready for instant action against hostile Indians on the upper Missouri. All of them looked extremely impressive as the sun caught their paddles and the smoke belched from their tall funnels.

For sixty years the steamboats of the Mississippi, the Missouri and other rivers of the West were a key part of the Western scene. Businessmen and everyday folk needed them for travel, for the transportation of cotton and other goods, and sometimes for carrying wounded back from bitter battles with Indians.

The first steamboat to trade between New Orleans and Natchez on the Mississippi set out on its maiden trip in 1811. By 1818 another boat laboriously puffed up part of the Missouri. By the 1840s, the Steamboat Age was at its peak. There were no less than 1,190 steamboats on Western rivers by 1846, and by the 1860s the lower Missouri was even busier than the mighty Mississippi herself. But the 70s saw steamboats lose trade to the railroads.

Most of the captains owned their boats and were kings of the rivers. They spent fortunes on furnishing their craft, knowing that they could recover their outlay and more in a single season. They were skilled rivermen who also acted as bankers and merchants. A plantation owner would hand over his whole stock of cotton or sugar and leave it to the captain to get the best market price for it.

The boats carried all sorts of travellers: soldiers, politicians, killers, gamblers, and respectable ladies and gentlemen. There was plenty of entertainment provided, including plays, and from the 1830s there were full-time showboats which gave performances afloat and ashore.

The steamboat 'Rosebud' on the Missouri (Denver Public Library, Western Hist. Dept.)

The pilots were almost as important as the captains, as a Western tale shows. Three men applied for the job of pilot on a particularly fine boat. The first two told the captain how they had never run aground or even hit a snag during twenty years on the river. The third applicant said: 'Cap'n, I reckon I know this river better than any man alive. I guess there ain't a snag, mudbank or sandbar that I ain't hit in my time.'

The captain at once grasped the pilot's hand and said: 'You're my man. You really *know* the river.'

Because many of the steamboats were woodburners, captains who were carrying cotton used to have up to eight men standing by, armed with water buckets to use on any sparks that hit the bales piled on the decks. Also, like the coalburners, the engines were liable to explode. A passenger told Charles Dickens in 1842, when the novelist was visiting the West, 'They generally blow up forward.' So the best accommodation tended to be at the stern.

Long after the great days of the Mississippi steamboats were over, there were still vessels on the upper Missouri, and some were sailing on the Yukon and its tributaries in the 1898 gold rush. But the steamboat's greatest moment came in 1876. On 27 June, 1876 a Crow Indian came on board the *Far West* to tell Captain Grant Marsh that not far from where the boat lay at anchor at the mouth of the Little Big Horn in Montana, General Custer and his entire command had been wiped out by the Sioux and Cheyennes. Next, General Terry appeared and ordered Captain Marsh to prepare to take on board fifty-two wounded men from other units that had taken part in the battle. He was to transport them 1,136 kilometres down the Big Horn, the raging, uncharted Yellowstone, and then the Missouri, to Fort Lincoln.

Captain Grant Marsh's epic nightmare journey through rough waters, with a stop to carry troops across river and a second stop to collect supplies, took from the evening of 3 July until 11 pm on 5 July travelling at an average of 560 kilometres a day. Because of the hectic speed, never again equalled, fifty-one of the wounded survived.

The Pony Express

WANTED—young, skinny, wiry fellows, not over 18. Must be expert riders, willing to risk death daily. Orphans preferred. Wages $25 a week. . . .

That notice appeared in a San Francisco paper in 1860. It started a brave, crazy interlude in Western history that stands apart from the story of transportation on the Frontier.

It was like a great relay race, with death as the loser's prize. It was expensive to run and out of date a year after it had started. Yet the saga of the Pony Express and its young riders who carried the mail over plains and mountains and through hostile Indian country, fired the world's imagination.

Gold-rich California badly needed a first-rate mail service in the 1850s to link up with the rest of the states 3,200 kilometres to the east. As late as 1857 John Butterfield's Overland Mail took twenty-two days to reach California using a route that swung far to the south. Yet many Californians were convinced a central mail route was possible and senators managed to persuade a transportation firm, Russell, Majors and Waddell, into starting one.

The three feared—rightly—that they would lose a fortune, but they set the mail service up in only sixty days, building 190 stations at regular intervals across the West. They purchased 500 fast, tough Indian ponies and hired eighty riders whose average age was eighteen. They decided to use seventy-five ponies in each direction for a mail run. At every station, the Pony Express rider would have just two minutes to move his saddlebags onto a fresh horse and set out again. After riding a fixed distance, one rider would hand over the mail to the next, and so it would continue until the end of the journey.

The Pony Express route followed the stage line to Salt Lake City, then hit a desert region of low hills, valleys and barren rocky country. It ended at Sacramento, state capital of California, where the mails were rushed by fast steamboat to San Francisco.

The riders had to be completely without fear and were not allowed to drink or swear. Each one was given a Bible to carry. Their saddles were light and the mail was confined to telegrams and letters that had to be written on thin paper enclosed by oilcloth as a protection against bad weather. The first run from St. Joseph, Missouri, on 3 April, 1860 took a mere ten days and the last rider got a terrific welcome as he galloped into Sacramento.

PONY EXPRESS !

CHANGE OF   REDUCED

TIME !   RATES !

10 Days to San Francisco!

LETTERS

WILL BE RECEIVED AT THE

OFFICE, 84 BROADWAY,

NEW YORK,

Up to **4** P. M. every TUESDAY,

AND

Up to **2½** P. M. every SATURDAY,

Which will be forwarded to connect with the PONY EXPRESS leaving
ST. JOSEPH, Missouri,

Every WEDNESDAY and SATURDAY at 11 P. M.

TELEGRAMS

Sent to Fort Kearney on the mornings of MONDAY and FRIDAY, will connect with **PONY** leaving St. Joseph, WEDNESDAYS and SATURDAYS.

EXPRESS CHARGES.

LETTERS weighing half ounce or under..............**$1 00**
For every additional half ounce or fraction of an ounce 1 00
In all cases to be enclosed in 10 cent Government Stamped Envelopes,
And all Express CHARGES Pre-paid.

☞ **PONY EXPRESS ENVELOPES For Sale at our Office.**

WELLS, FARGO & CO., Ag'ts.

New York, Ju'y 1. 1861.

The Pony Express was the most glamorous mail service ever (Author's Collection)

Buffalo Bill (William F. Cody) brought his fabulous Wild West show to Britain several times, a big attraction being the authentic Deadwood Stage in which visitors to the show could ride if they were lucky. Cody stands in front, and on the box is another ex-scout and tall story-teller, John Nelson (Denver Public Library, Western Hist. Dept.)

When the mail reached San Francisco a grand parade celebrated the event.

Depending on the terrain, the riders covered between 56 and 120 kilometres a day. They had to average 14 kilometres an hour and some achieved 32. One team got through in only six days.

Though the ponies were so fleet that they could usually outstrip Indians, the stations the riders headed for were often attacked. It was in and around them that most of the Pony Express's casualties occurred.

Incredibly, most riders got through safely, despite every hazard, human, animal and natural. Most, but not all. One pony reached a Nevada station with its rider slumped dead over the saddle horn, and his body thick with arrows. So tightly was the dead youth clutching the mane of his horse that it had to be cut from his grasp. And the mail was intact.

One young rider was later to become world famous. This was

Billy Cody, the future Buffalo Bill, hunter, army scout, Indian fighter, and, finally, a showman in charge of his own spectacular Wild West show. His nickname came from the enormous number of buffalo he killed. He was a Pony Express rider when only fourteen, but he was not the youngest. 'Bronco Charlie' Miller, who later performed in Buffalo Bill's show, and survived to be 105, rode when he was only eleven!

After only eighteen months, the Pony Express collapsed and its three creators were ruined men. The main reason for the catastrophe was the completion of the trans-continental telegraph line which linked West and East more rapidly than the fastest riders ever could. Also the operation cost far more than could be charged for the service. When the service ended on 26 October, 1861 34,753 items of mail had been carried.

Stagecoach Saga

One summer morning in 1865 a band of Sioux attacked a stagecoach on the Nebraska plains. They were armed with bows and arrows, which should have been enough to bring the stage to a sudden halt. But the guard, riding shotgun on top of the coach, kept the red men at a distance and forced them to give up the chase.

This shotgun was no ordinary Westerner: he was the head of the stage line, Ben Holladay, who believed in seeing things for himself. On this occasion he had set out to prove that travel by stagecoach could begin again in the West now that the Civil War was over. Where better to find out the facts than from the top of a stagecoach! When he wasn't riding shotgun, he sometimes drove his own coaches.

The stagecoach was the best means of communication in the West, except where there were navigable rivers; that was until the 1890s when a whole network of railroads criss-crossed the West.

Travelling by stage was not as dangerous as it is often portrayed. Badmen who held up stagecoaches could not be sure of succeeding against a coachload of up to eighteen people, some of them heavily armed, for that was how many could be crammed onto the Concord coach, the Queen of the Prairies, along with their baggage and, possibly, gold.

Not that it was a comfy way to travel, even if there was not a full load of passengers, for proper roads were non-existent. The *Omaha Herald* warned on 3 October, 1877: 'Don't imagine for a moment that you are going on a picnic. Expect annoyances, discomfort and some hardship.'

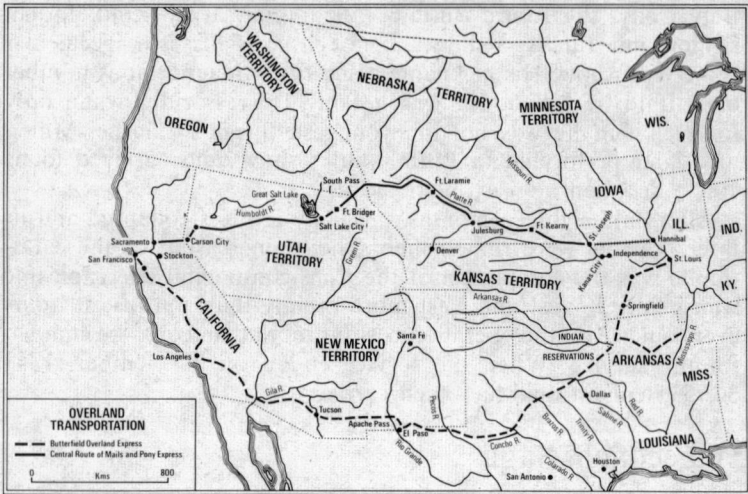

Western stage lines

Other useful information included:

> In very cold weather abstain entirely from liquor when on the road; because you will freeze twice as quickly when under its influence. . . . Don't smoke a strong pipe inside the coach—spit on the leeward side. . . . Never shoot on the road as the noise might frighten the horses. Don't discuss politics or religion. Don't point out where murders have been committed especially if there are women passengers.

The first stagecoach king to rule the West was John Butterfield, who graduated from driving a stage in New York State to becoming the biggest name in staging in the East and also a power in the steamboat world. In 1857 he founded the American Express Company and the next year was given government permission to organise the first transcontinental stage line.

This line stretched from St. Louis, Missouri, to Los Angeles and San Francisco, California, sweeping down into the Southwest and through Apache country, a distance of 4,480 kilometres in all. Butterfield set up stations every 32 kilometres, complete with wells, and hired 1,000 men, 1,800 horses and 250 coaches. His line ran twice a week and the journey usually took twenty-five days and cost about £50 in today's money. Each passenger was allowed

18 kilos of baggage but no gold was ever carried by Butterfield coaches, which cut down visits from 'road agents.'

The first run of all took only twenty-three days, the first dust-covered stagecoach rumbling into the tiny town of Tipton, Missouri, in 1858 ready to deposit its passengers at the railhead for their trip to the East. Within three years Butterfield was carrying more mail than ships sailing from the Atlantic to the Pacific via Cape Horn. The Pony Express might be far faster in its short glorious day, but the bulk of mail was still carried in coaches, whose prices were cheaper anyway.

The drivers of stagecoaches were a rugged, colourful breed, rejoicing in splendid names like 'Cherokee' Bill, 'Sage Brush' Charlie and 'One-eyed' Charlie Parkhurst, 'the greatest whip in the West'. Charlie was held up one day by a bandit called 'Sugar-Foot' and decided to become a six-gun expert. Next time they met, Sugar-Foot came off second best. When pistol-packing, baccy-chomping Charlie Parkhurst died in 1879 a strange discovery was made. Charlie was a woman.

Ben Holladay bought up Butterfield's empire and was soon providing lines to booming mining towns and frontier communities. He never stopped travelling on his own line to keep things up to standard. But in 1866 he suddenly decided that railroads were the transport of the future, sold up his company and started laying 'iron roads'.

He sold his company to the famous firm of Wells, Fargo, collecting a fortune and a directorship of the company. Henry Wells and William Fargo, who had come up the hard way in the East, and then built their empire up in the Californian gold rush, now found themselves in charge of the world's greatest stagecoach network. When railroads threatened them they went into railroads themselves and into banking.

Rails West

The great man aimed a hearty blow at the golden spike below him and missed. He handed the sledgehammer to another eminent personage, who had a splitting headache and missed also. The telegraph operator could wait no longer. The first blows were meant to have triggered off three dots, for the spike was linked by a wire to the telegraph. Quickly the operator tapped out three dots and all over the United States the celebrations began. Bells pealed, guns boomed and locomotive whistles pierced the air. At last the continent was spanned by rail.

The date was 10 May, 1869 and the place was Promontory Point, just north of Salt Lake City, Utah.

Two companies had built the railroad, the Central Pacific eastwards from California and the Union Pacific westwards from Omaha, Nebraska. Each used thousands of workers. Many of the C.P.'s were lightly dressed Chinese, who suffered terribly in the mountains and snows, and many of the U.P.'s were Irish. But the work crews were a very international bunch altogether. There were tough Civil War veterans, freed black slaves, Indians, Mormons, Britons and Germans, and they laid 3 to 8 kilometres a day, running trestles over rivers, forcing their way through mountains and filling in ravines.

The ex-soldiers came in handy when Indians attacked the U.P. crews. The more peaceful Indians in the far West caused little trouble. But so fiercely did the Sioux and Cheyennes resent the crossing of their lands by the railroads that they kept up steady attacks on the workers, especially isolated advance parties and bridge-builders. They sometimes ripped up rails, tore down telegraph poles and even attacked trains. By 1868 there were as many as 5,000 soldiers needed to guard the railroad and its crews.

Soon, other railroads were completed, and by 1900 there were no less than five transcontinental lines and many more local ones.

The Central Pacific from the West met the Union Pacific from the East and at last the United States was spanned by rail (Union Pacific Railroad)

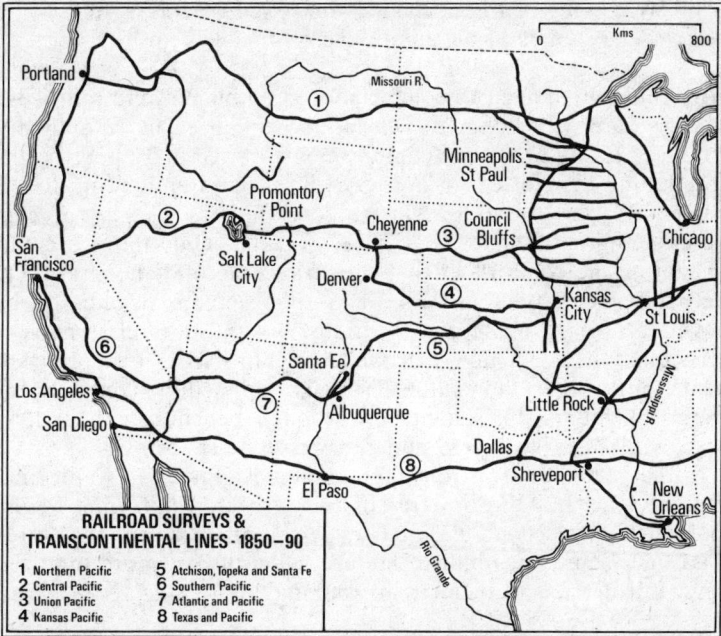

**RAILROAD SURVEYS &
TRANSCONTINENTAL LINES · 1850—90**

1	Northern Pacific	5	Atchison, Topeka and Santa Fe
2	Central Pacific	6	Southern Pacific
3	Union Pacific	7	Atlantic and Pacific
4	Kansas Pacific	8	Texas and Pacific

And behind the railroad came the settlers, thousands, then millions of them, from the Eastern states and from Europe, for now it was easy to go West, or at least to the parts of the West served by the railroads.

Not that the railroads' advertising departments felt obliged to mention that the living was not easy in the West. Some stressed the joys of the northern Plains, but naturally made no mention of the cruel winters, others made the whole West sound like the Garden of Eden. And one showed that Kansas had 'quietened down some' since the wild Texan boys had been on the rampage. In 1888 the Chicago, Kansas and Nebraska Railway claimed that Northern Kansas was the 'finest country in the world' to which a man could bring his family and discover 'fertile lands, prosperous towns, plenty of churches and schools and NO SALOONS'. Wild Bill Hickok and friends would not have recognised the place.

What was the greatest load of cotton bales ever carried by a Mississippi steamboat?
In 1881 the *Henry Frank* carried 9,226 bales. Back in 1811, the first steamboat in the West, the *New Orleans,* would have taken a whole season to transport that many.

What were some of the nicknames for a stagecoach driver?
Whip, Whipster, Jehu or Charlie were four of them.

Who contributed most to comfortable travel on Western railroads?
George Mortimer Pullman, whose innovations included splendid dining cars, day and night compartments, which had upper berths that could be slotted into the ceilings, and much improved accommodation for those who could afford it. His parlour cars were like miniature Victorian drawing rooms. Only the rich could pay for all the comforts of first-class travel. Second-class travellers were not given any luxuries, but had upholstered seats and at least travelled as part of the express trains, but the third-class passengers, many of them newly arrived emigrants from Europe, were treated little better than cattle. True, they crossed the continent for about 40 dollars, but on narrow wooden benches, with endless stops while they waited to allow expresses to shoot by.

In the 1880s the trip from the junction at Omaha to California, (roughly the 3,200 kilometres of the Oregon/California Trails) took first- and second-class passengers four days, but the third-class ones sometimes had to endure a journey of more than ten days. But it was still better than walking!

8
INDIAN-FIGHTING ARMY

There was Sergeant John McCaffery
    and Captain Donohue
They make us march and toe the mark,
    in gallant Company 'Q'.
Oh the drums would roll, upon my soul,
    This is the style we'd go,
Forty miles a day, on beans and hay,
    In the Regular Army O.

Forty miles a day—64 kilometres—on beans and hay! Sometimes it was much further. After the huge volunteer army had been dispersed in 1865 at the end of the Civil War, a mere 15,000 officers and men were stationed in the West, responsible for the colossal area stretching from the Mississippi to the Pacific.

And the task of these few soldiers was basically impossible, for the army was ordered to play a double role, to protect the Indian and fight him, sometimes at almost the same moment. For instance, the army would be ordered to attack, and seize the Indians' land, but would soon find itself trying to keep intruders off it, especially if gold was found there. It was made harder because successive governments did not know how to solve the 'Indian problem', or would reverse the previous orders, usually for the worse. In these circumstances, they did what soldiers always have to do, obeyed orders.

Fighting took up only part of a soldier's life. Most of the time, especially before the Civil War when communications were appalling, the main enemy was boredom. An enlisted man got a wretched sixteen dollars a month, which was reduced to thirteen in the 1870s. And promotion for officers seemed to get worse, not better. A lieutenant, who had led a regiment in the Civil War as a colonel, might take twenty years to become a captain. The smallness of the army was much to blame. An officer had to be dedicated to endure such a lack of prospects. Service was for five years and, fortunately for the army, many of the best soldiers signed on several times.

After the war the West was divided into the Departments of Columbia, California, Dakota, Arizona, Missouri, the Platte and Texas. In each there were small forts of stone or wood. Only a handful of forts had two-storey buildings. Most were a collection of huts, usually overcrowded and almost always too hot in the summer and cold in winter. Few had pallisades around them, except some older ones, for Indians had too much sense to attack forts. A garrison might contain as many as two hundred men or as few as ten or twelve in a small post beside the overland telegraph.

In a fort the soldier could expect more than beans, but unless the local hunting was good he was faced with a dreary menu: salt pork, salt beef, dried vegetables and fruit, hardtack (hard biscuits), molasses, coffee, and bread if there was a post baker. And there was whisky.

There were few women. Before the Civil War only officers' wives were allowed in a fort, so the enlisted man had to hope he was posted near a town or settlement. After the war, however, the wives and families of other ranks sometimes came West with their husbands.

Popular pastimes were horse-racing, dancing—no girl would ever be short of partners—hunting, reading, and visiting the sutler's store, which, apart from selling goods, was a sort of club for officers and men. The life drove many to drink.

The soldiers, as opposed to the officers who were mainly American born, came from all parts of the world. There were many Irish, Germans, Swedes, English, Scots, Welsh, Swiss and other nationalities, as well as native Americans. Some of the Americans had fought for the South in the Civil War, but were now fighting alongside their old enemies.

The Cavalry was the strongest arm in the West, though many infantry regiments also served there. The famous Seventh Cavalry, Custer's outfit, were raised in 1866 and soon there were three additional regiments; the Ninth and the Tenth being black regiments. Their white officers were fiercely proud of their men's behaviour in many a ferocious fight. In action, cavalrymen more often than not fought on foot because then their aim was far more accurate and they could shoot faster. But like all soldiers in the West, much of their job was routine—wood-cutting, road-building, escort duty, and the inevitable drill.

There was no respite for them in the winter if a campaign was still being fought. That was an advantage they had over the Indians who had to remain in their camps. If they ventured out they could not move fast in the snow; if they stayed in, they might starve; but the army, thanks to the railroads, could wage winter warfare. Not that it made service any more popular. Nearly every year in the 1870s and 80s hundreds of men deserted, unable to endure the rugged life and the perils of Indian-fighting.

The soldiers were aided by civilian guides and Indian scouts, many of them from smaller tribes like the Crows and the Shoshones who were hostile to the Sioux and Cheyennes and who thought they had a better chance of survival on the American side. Later, defeated Indians, even Apaches, joined the Americans. Without the Apache guides the army would have never caught up with Apaches on the warpath. Joining the enemy was not usually considered treachery, for every Indian was entitled to do as he pleased, so fierce was the Indian love of liberty and freedom of choice. Besides, anything was better than eking out life on a barren reservation.

The Apaches could outstrip the cavalry in a day's march, partly because they rode their horses to death if necessary. Cavalry horses were tough creatures, big and strong and bred in the West. Most of the soldiers were tough, too, but there were always arrogant officers who knew nothing of Indian-fighting, and who led their men into traps, learning too late that their despised enemies were wiser than they realised.

Neither red men nor white men took many prisoners and many a soldier held back one bullet to kill himself rather than fall into enemy hands and be tortured. As racial tension rose, so atrocity bred atrocity. As for the wounded, those who were carried to safety had to endure rough conditions in field hospitals, though diseases such as smallpox, typhoid, tuberculosis and pneumonia killed more men than arrows ever did. But arrow wounds were more dangerous than the average bullet, which might pass straight through the body. Drawing out an arrow often caused it to break up in the wound.

The average soldier was far less anti-Indian than most Westerners, who agreed with General Sheridan that the only good Indians were dead ones. The Regulars simply got on with their unpleasant job, many of them respecting their valiant foes, and often sympathising with them. One of the Regulars wrote this about them:

> If I were an Indian, I think that I would greatly prefer to cast my lot among those of my people who adhered to the free open plains, rather than submit to the quiet, unexciting, uneventful life of a reservation.

His name was George Armstrong Custer.

George Armstrong Custer, glory-hunter (National Archives)

Who were the Buffalo Soldiers?

They were the black troops who served in four regiments of the army. They were given their nickname by the Indians, probably because they saw a resemblance between the soldiers' hair and the shaggy coat of the buffalo. The blacks were regarded very highly as fighters by the Indians.

How many soldiers were killed between 1865 and 1898 in the West?

59 officers and 860 other ranks. Many of the Indian 'wars' were little more than skirmishes.

Two opinions of General Custer

'A man respected and beloved by his followers, who would freely follow him into the "jaws of hell".' Mark Kellogg, war correspondent. 'He was often too hard on the men and the horses. He changed his mind too often. He was always right. He never conferred enough with his officers. When he got a notion, we had to go.' Jacob Horner, Private, Seventh Cavalry.

The second is the more usual opinion.

9
INDIAN EPIC

Where today are the Pequot? Where are the Narragansett, the Mohican, the Pokanoket, and many other once powerful tribes of our people? They have vanished before the greed and the oppression of the White Man, as snow before a summer sun.

Will we let ourselves be destroyed in our turn without a struggle, give up our homes, our country bequeathed to us by the Great Spirit, the graves of our dead and everything that is dear and sacred to us? I know you will cry with me, 'Never! Never!'

Chief Tecumseh of the Shawnees
who died in action in 1813

It was impossible for the Indians to win the last battle, for the odds were stacked against them. Their doom was sealed from the moment the first white pioneer settlers crossed the Appalachian Mountains in the East in the 1770s. The red men were destined to be driven ever westward, or wiped from the face of the earth. By the 1790s they had lost the old Northwest, including all of present-day Michigan, Ohio and Indiana, and forty years later, the Plains Indians were due for the same treatment as their brothers in the East. The nightmare was repeating itself.

The First Americans

Some 20,000 or 30,000 years ago wave after wave of Asians began crossing the Bering Straits into America and heading southwards. The crossing now is a mere 90 kilometres, with stepping-stone islands in between, and sometimes the gap is frozen over. In prehistoric times there was no strait at all, but a land bridge. The peoples penetrated to the very tip of South America, and some tribes, notably the Aztecs of Mexico and the Incas of Peru, produced extraordinary civilisations. But nothing to equal those civilisations appeared in what became the United States. When Columbus sailed westwards in 1492 there may have been some million or so 'Indians'. Their name stems from a simple mistake made by Columbus: he thought he had reached India. Nowadays, the word Amerind is often used to correct the mistake.

Indians are not 'red', most of them are brown. The first white men who landed in the East came across Indians who were fairly

Young Blackfoot brave, 1889 (The Commissioner, Royal Canadian Mounted Police)

light skinned. When they tanned their skin became reddish and then a splendid copper colour.

The Indians of 1492 were Stone Age warriors and farmers and, as we have seen, they were without the horse. In fact, the word 'Indian' is as vague and misleading as 'European' and 'Asian', for there were so many different life styles. But nearly every tribe, from the lowly Diggers of the Far West to advanced peoples like the Iroquois in the East, shared some things in common.

The Indian worshipped the Sun and the Earth, which was his mother. He did not own the Earth, for how could he own his mother? Of course, tribes had their own areas, especially where the art of farming had been learned, and hunting rights were violently disputed. That was not surprising for most Indians loved fighting. But there was never land ownership, land *hunger*, in the white sense. Land was held in sacred trust by a whole people. This was one of the many causes of trouble between red men and white.

If the Indian loved fighting and prized bravery in battle highly, it must not be thought that his life was one long round of warfare. The Indians loved—and still love—family life and an Indian child had a marvellous time. By our standards he was thoroughly spoiled. Discipline came later.

Some tribes, especially in the East, practised torture, but sometimes the Indian use of it was almost religious, a form of escape from tension and troubles more than revenge. The wives of slain warriors sometimes tortured from motives of pure revenge. It is hard to understand the Iroquois attitude to torture, for the victim was honoured and if he could last out for a long time and sing defiance at his captors he was even more admired.

The Iroquois lived in the Eastern woodlands and forests and had a democratic form of government that many Americans admired. Across the Mississippi most tribes hunted, on foot, the buffalo, which gave them food, shelter and clothing, while their dogs dragged their few belongings. Some led simple lives as primitive farmers.

The coming of the horse revolutionised tribe after tribe, and by the mid-eighteenth century the Plains Indians had become superb horsemen. The buffalo hunt was transformed, for now it was a far more exciting event. But the greatest game of all, even more exciting than war, was horse-stealing. Like medieval knights, the Plains Indians developed a code of conduct that did them no good when they began to fight the white men. For instance, it was considered finer to touch an enemy—to 'count coup' on him—

than to kill him, which was no way to take on Americans, many of whom were anxious to exterminate the Indians.

The Plains Indians did not suffer at first. When legendary Mountain Men like Jim Bridger and Kit Carson were roaming the West no one wanted the Indian's land. Gold had not yet been found in California and the Indians were not yet 'in the way'. But the danger signals were there. It was not simply what had happened far to the East, where whole tribes had died of white diseases and bullets, or been forced westwards or onto wretched reservations. Terrible things began to happen in the South.

In the South there dwelt tribes who had outstripped even the Iroquois, to whom they were related. These were the Five Civilised Tribes, the Cherokees, Choctaws, Creeks, Chickasaws and Seminoles, and in the 1820s and 1830s they were forced to abandon their homes and settle in Indian Territory, now Oklahoma. The key figure in this tragedy was Andrew Jackson, a typical Indian-hating Westerner who became President of the United States in 1828. He wanted every Indian out of the Southeast, even those who had fought with him against the British and other Indians.

A number of 'trails of tears' followed, the worst of which happened to the Cherokees. These Indians were educated to the point where nearly all could read and write, because one of their tribe called Sequoyah had invented an alphabet. They had a higher standard of living than the poor white men who surrounded them, and the Supreme Court of the United States backed their claims to stay in their homeland, the state of Georgia.

But gold had been found in Georgia in the late 1820s. This helped seal their doom. The anti-Indian President simply overruled the Supreme Court and in 1838 and 1839 the Cherokees were moved by force to Indian Territory. 4,000 out of 13,000 Cherokees died and only a few hundred escaped exile by hiding in the mountains of North Carolina where their descendants live to this day.

The story of these removals of whole tribes is almost unbearable to read. Never believe that Indians don't cry. Many did when they were forced from their homes. One old Creek who had fought for the Americans in his time was removed with the rest. On his last night in his native land he spent the final moments alone, then in the morning said to a white friend: 'Last evening I saw the sun set for the last time, and its light shine upon the treetops, and the land, and the water, that I am never to look upon again.' Then the old man walked away without looking round, heading westwards.

Quanah Parker, the last great chief of the Comanches. His mother was a captured white girl who pined away when she was 'rescued' by the Americans (Smithsonian Institution)

But there was one southern tribe that refused to move. The Seminoles of Florida were determined to die rather than move, and they had geography on their side. Some of the tribe had already gone west to Indian Territory, but the rest fought in the swamps and wastes of Florida like tigers and could not be beaten.

There were three Seminole Wars and the United States spent $20 million and lost 1,500 men trying to subdue a phantom enemy in nightmarish campaigns. The greatest Seminole leader was Osceola, an unconquerable guerilla fighter who was finally caught by treachery under a flag of truce, to die later in prison.

Many army officers sympathised with the Indians. One wrote: 'No Seminole proves false to his country, nor has a single instance ever occurred of a first-rate warrior having surrendered.' Wrote another: 'Five years ago I came to Florida as a volunteer, willingly making every effort in my power to be of service in punishing, as I thought, the Indians. I now come, with the persuasion that the Indians have been wronged.'

The wars ended in 1842. Some Seminoles decided to join the other Seminoles and the rest of the Civilised Tribes in the West. Others remained unconquered in the swamps known as the Everglades. Huge sums were offered them to move, but they refused. Their descendants are still there.

Life and Death on the Plains

On the Plains were the Indians of everyone's imagination, to such an extent that many of today's Indians, who have no link with the Plains, dress like the Sioux, Cheyennes, Arapahoes and the other famous tribes on ceremonial occasions.

Plains Indians were dreamers of dreams on the vast, windy, empty plains, and the coming of the horse made them doubly so. They saw visions, believed in good medicine and bad medicine. Their ancestors had been slow movers; some had been farmers on the edge of the forests; now, with the coming of the horse, most of them were nomads, horses dragging their lodge poles which were the basic structures of their tipis. Buffalo hides made the tipi a home.

Life in camp was governed by rules and so was the buffalo hunt.Members of warrior societies wore special costumes and behaved in set ways, for war was formal on the Plains. Some tribes scalped victims, but not all. The habit had spread from the East where white men gave bounty money for scalps as tokens of death. There was less torture on the Plains than in the forests, though it existed.

These proud, religious peoples went in for the self torture of the Sun Dance which was a sacred ritual. Many Indians were in a religious trance during the ordeal. Skewers were thrust through the brave's chest flesh and attached to ropes, by which he hung until at last the skewers broke free from him.

The Sioux, perhaps the most famous of all Indians, were really a confederacy of seven tribes called the Dakota. The word Dakota means 'allies'. 'Sioux' was a French version of an Algonquin Indian term meaning 'enemies,' or, more accurately, 'serpents'. Their first major uprising occurred in Minnesota in 1862, when the Civil War was raging and there were few soldiers available to combat it.

The Minnesota Sioux, the most easterly of the Dakota confederacy, consisted of four sub-tribes called the Santee, and they had plenty of reason to be angry. Nearly every Indian war was triggered off by white men and this was no exception, for the Santee had suffered from land grabs, shortage of promised food and unscrupulous traders and agents. One agent was heard to sneer: 'If they're hungry, let them eat grass!'

The uprising, one of the most ferocious in Western history, was led by a chief called Little Crow. He knew the power of the white men and had begun to follow their ways, but when the crisis came he did not hesitate.

Minnesota was farming country, thick with settlers, and the slaughter was terrible. 700 settlers died, many of them harmless folk who paid for the follies of their government and officials; 100 soldiers, too, were killed in the fighting. When the army moved in strength against the Santees the rebellion finally collapsed. Little Crow was shot, many chiefs and braves were hanged, and the Santees were driven westwards to the Dakotas, except for some who escaped to Canada where they were allowed to stay.

For almost thirty years warfare was to rage on the Plains, with a few short intervals of peace. If the Little Crow war had angered the white men, the Indians were inflamed still more by the worst white atrocity in the history of the West. This was the Sand Creek Massacre, perpetrated in 1864 on peaceful Cheyennes of Chief Black Kettle's band by the bloodthirsty Reverend J. N. Chivington and his Colorado volunteers. Some 200 women and children were killed, and seventy or so mainly unarmed men, and some Arapahoes also died in the slaughter.

There have always been some to justify the white men, claiming that the Cheyenne braves were away on the warpath on the day

Red Cloud, a great Sioux chief, who won a major war against the United States (National Archives)

of the massacre, and that Indians had killed hundreds of settlers. But it is fact that Black Kettle longed for peace and was camped at Sand Creek on the advice of the military. It is fact that Chivington had urged his men on by saying, 'Kill and scalp all, big and little: nits make lice.' It is fact that although Black Kettle escaped, his friend White Antelope did not. Instead he stood in front of his lodge singing his death song—'Nothing lives long, except the earth and the mountains,' and went on singing until bullets cut him down.

The volunteer soldiers were welcomed back in Denver, carrying grisly trophies with them, but most Americans were sickened. And the massacre had a single result, more bloodshed.

The most dramatic of the many wars that followed soon after Sand Creek was Red Cloud's war, which the Indians won.

It was triggered off when the whites decided to protect the Bozeman Trail, which ran from Fort Laramie, Wyoming, to the goldfields of Montana, by building a road and a series of forts. Some Indians had already given in, and even the great warrior, Red Cloud, was willing to talk to the white commissioners when he thought that the road was to be a peaceful one.

Just as it looked as if he might sign on behalf of the Oglala Sioux, into Fort Laramie rode Colonel Henry Carrington and 700 officers and men. Furiously, Red Cloud rose and said: 'The Great White Father sends us presents and wants us to sell him the road, but before the Indians say yes or no White Chief goes with soldiers to steal the road.' Then he stalked out and many chiefs and braves went with him.

The biggest of the forts along the trail was Fort Phil Kearny. Raiding Sioux and Cheyennes made its construction something of a running battle, but the major action occurred in December 1866.

In the fort was Captain Fetterman, an arrogant hothead from the East who knew nothing of Indian warfare and despised the enemy. Several times he boasted: 'Give me eighty men and I'll ride through the whole Sioux Nation.' Finally, he got his wish on 21 December.

A lookout on a hill outside the fort signalled that a wood-gathering party was under attack and Carrington reluctantly gave the fire-eating Fetterman permission to ride to their rescue. He rode out, not with eighty but eighty-one men.

It was a trap, of course, for a band of picked warriors, one of them a young Oglala brave called Crazy Horse, lured Fetterman beyond the safety limit—despite Carrington's instructions—and straight into a huge war party of Sioux, Cheyennes and Arapahoes. There were no survivors.

Fort Phil Kearny was too strong for the Indians to attack, though the 'Fetterman Massacre', as it came to be called, ensured that an unpleasant Christmas was endured by all. (Indian victories were almost always called massacres by whites.)

Revenge of a sort for the American soldiers came some months later when on two occasions their new rapid-fire, breach-loading rifles played havoc with the unsuspecting Indians. Yet Red Cloud won his war, and in 1868 the troops were ordered out of the Powder River country, where most of it had been fought, and also out of the Black Hills 'forever'. Red Cloud was the only Western chief to win a long war against the United States, and his men had the grim satisfaction of seeing the soldiers march away. Then Fort Phil Kearny was burnt to the ground.

Red Cloud never went on the warpath again, standing aloof in the Custer campaign and the final tragedy at Wounded Knee. He paid a spectacular visit to Washington and New York, gaining much sympathy for the Indian cause.

But out West the attitude remained the same—remove or exterminate the Indian. The process was hastened by the virtual extermination of the buffalo, first to feed railroad builders, then

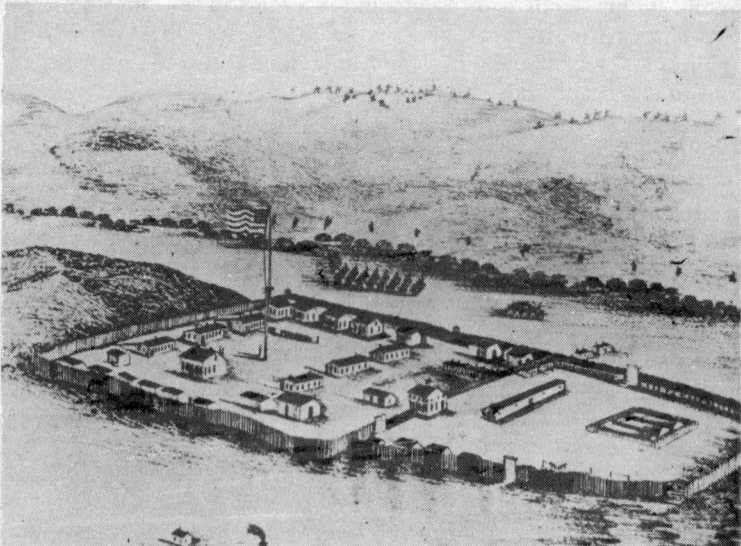

Fort Phil Kearny, Wyoming, was the scene of desperate fighting in Red Cloud's War. In 1868 the Indians burnt it to the ground (Wyoming State Archives & Hist. Dept.)

for their hides and bones. And it was soon realised that the Indians would be forced to submit if their greatest asset was killed off, so the slaughter went on. By 1889 there were only 541 buffalo left alive. And even more disastrous than the destruction of the buffalo for the Indians was the flood of white settlers who poured onto the plains and prairies in the 1870s and 1880s, brought West by the railroads.

Yet it was gold which was to bring about the greatest confrontation between the Sioux and the American, gold in the sacred Black Hills. Into the Black Hills in 1874 rode an expedition which was allegedly making a military and scientific survey. The leader was Colonel, acting General, George Custer, who had been a 'Golden-Boy' General in the Civil War, making his name in the final battles as a dashing cavalry commander. Vain, ambitious, but undoubtedly brave, with his long hair and wide-brimmed slouch hat, he was known as a harsh commander who had as many enemies as admirers. If, as we saw earlier, he had some sympathy with the Indians, he was too much of a glory hunter to let that stop him fighting them ruthlessly. At the Battle of the Washita on a bitterly cold night in 1868 he had attacked a Cheyenne camp whose chief was the wretched Black Kettle of Sand Creek fame. This time the much-wronged Indian died, along with many women and children.

Custer found plenty of evidence of gold in the Black Hills and broadcast the news on his return. The result was a stampede, with the government powerless to keep the prospectors out. An offer of cash was made to the Indians for the Black Hills. Red Cloud, now 'tame', was willing to negotiate, but younger men like Sitting Bull, Crazy Horse and Gall were not. The stage was set for the most famous Indian fight of them all.

In the bitter winter of 1875, those Sioux who had left their reservations because they did not feel bound by treaties they had not signed were ordered to return to them. Most of them refused, and the following year a three-pronged invasion of Indian country was launched, General Gibbon marching from eastern Montana, General Crook from further south and Custer heading west from the Missouri.

The first Indian victory was against Crook's men, who were outfought in the valley of the Rosebud by Sioux led by their greatest warrior, Crazy Horse. Then, on 25 June, Custer's men stumbled on the great encampment of Sioux, Cheyennes and some Arapahoes.

Without waiting for his fellow generals, Custer decided to finish the war himself, sealing his own fate by dividing his command. While Major Reno and Captain Benteen were ordered to the flanks, Custer and some two hundred men headed straight to their destruction in the valley through which the Little Big Horn flowed. The Indians were taken by surprise, but only for a moment. Some 3,000 warriors or more wiped out the Americans in a furious fight that lasted no more than an hour. No one knows what happened for certain that blazing day, for few Indians talked about the battle until years later for fear of reprisals and few had known at first who had attacked them. Besides, a thick pall of gunsmoke hung over the battlefield.

The rest of the Seventh had no idea what had happened, being pinned down by other Indians. When the news broke on the outside world 40 million Americans were celebrating the one hundredth anniversary of their country, for they heard about the fight on 4 July 1876.

Sadly for the victors, the battle was to be their Last Stand as well as Custer's. The U.S. Army moved relentlessly against the hostiles. Sitting Bull fled to Canada with many of his followers, remaining there until forced to ride south in 1881.

By then Crazy Horse had been murdered, the valiant, handsome

Chief Big Foot's frozen body lying in the snow at Wounded Knee, where he and so many of his band were killed in 1890 in the last battle of the Indian Wars (National Archives)

Crazy Horse who at the Little Big Horn had called to his men: 'Today is a good day to fight! Today is a good day to die!'

Despair now overtook the once mighty Sioux as they endured the wretchedness of reservation life. Then, far to the west in Nevada a Paiute Indian named Wovoka had a vision of a fast approaching time when the buffalo would return and the white man would vanish from the West. The Great Spirit would see to these things and had given his people a dance that, though a simple shuffle, was big medicine. It was called the Ghost Dance.

This new religion spread all over the West. It was a message of peace, but not to the Sioux. For them it was a war dance, and by wearing Ghost Dance shirts they thought they would be safe from white men's bullets. The result was a double tragedy. With rumours of a major Indian uprising sweeping the United States, Sitting Bull was killed by Indian police who had been sent to arrest him. Then, at Wounded Knee, the Seventh Cavalry got its revenge for the Little Big Horn when the band of Chief Big Foot was almost wiped out in the snow by rifle and artillery fire. It was December 1890 and the last battle of the Indian Wars. The Ghost Shirts had failed.

Elsewhere, other tribes had fought even more bitterly than the Sioux. Space does not allow details of these tragic wars, but one tribe cannot be left out of even the shortest account—the unconquerable Apaches.

Captain Jack, who led the Modocs in a brilliant campaign against the U.S. Army in 1872-3. He ended up on the gallows (Smithsonian Institution)

Chief Joseph of the Nez Percés. With his people he made a retreat of over 3,000 kilometres, pursued by 5,000 soldiers. They were forced to surrender near the Canadian border and were then sent to rot on a barren reservation. This noblest of Indian chiefs was greatly admired by his enemies. (Smithsonian Institution, National Anthropoligical Archives)

The Apaches

Apaches! Incredibly, considering their fame, there were probably never more than 6,000 of them, and they were split up into tribes who only occasionally united to fight as one. The very word Apache tells us much about them, for it is a Zuni Indian word meaning—enemy!

Hated by many other Southwestern tribes and by the Mexicans, these unbelievably ferocious guerilla fighters were heroic figures who fought like fiends to survive. And if the Americans, both government and people, had treated them honourably, there would never have been the savage series of struggles known as the Apache Wars.

The Apaches were human tigers of the desert who never regarded war as the greatest of all games, as the Sioux and the Cheyennes tended to do. They could live off even the barest deserts like lizards, could run 64 kilometres a day and ride more than twice as far.

Their ferocity had been noted with feeling by the Spaniards, but it grew with the years, so bitterly did the Mexicans and Apaches hate each other. The Mexicans used extermination tactics: mass murder, the grossest treachery, and bounty hunters who were paid by results. The Apaches repaid in kind.

There was no reason for the Apaches to feel that the Americans were enemies at first, especially as they shared a common enemy in the Mexicans. Then, in 1853, Mexico sold the United States a vast tract of land in what is now southern Arizona and southern New Mexico, and the Apaches found themselves classed as Americans, though no one had bothered to consult them.

In 1861, Chief Cochise of the Chiricahua Apaches, who had tried to remain at peace with the Americans, was wrongly accused by a foolish young army officer of kidnapping a white boy. Furiously, he joined his father-in-law, Chief Mangas Coloradas, who had already been forced onto the warpath by white men's treatment of himself and his people. A twenty-six-year nightmare began.

They waged a ruthless campaign to drive every white out of the Southwest or into his grave.

'Exterminate the Apache!' became government policy, but that was easier ordered than done. Except when the Indians found themselves up against artillery for the first time, Cochise was invincible, especially during the Civil War when many troops were withdrawn to fight in the East. At one time he lorded it over all

Geronimo, the most famous of all Apaches, posing ferociously in 1886 (Smithsonian Institution, National Anthropological Archives)

Arizona, except for the beleaguered town of Tucson.

In 1863, Mangas Coloradas, now old and tired, was caught by a trick and murdered 'attempting to escape'. This made Cochise, still secretly longing for peace, and knowing that dead Apaches could not be replaced, even more ruthless.

Peace finally came to the Chiricahuas because Cochise trusted a frontiersman named Tom Jeffords, who had earlier risked his life by riding into Cochise's impregnable stronghold to ask the chief if he would allow mail-riders through Apache territory, for Jeffords's men were being killed in droves and something had to be done. To ride into the stronghold seemed suicidal, but Cochise was impressed and agreed to let the harmless mail men through. He and Jeffords became blood brothers, and when the tall, bearded American, who knew of Cochise's longing for peace, led a deeply religious, one-armed Civil War hero named General O. O. Howard to see the great chief, the result was an end to the slaughter.

This could have been the end of the Apache Wars, for Cochise was given his beloved Chiricahua Mountains as a reservation and Tom Jeffords became his agent. Yet only two years after the chief died in 1874, the government, giving in to those who wanted to grab the mountains for themselves, ordered the Chiricahuas to go to the grim, unhealthy San Carlos Reservation to rot with other Apache bands. In disgust Jeffords at once resigned from his post.

Then followed years of bitter guerilla warfare as bands left the reservations on daring, bloody raids on both sides of the border. The most spectacular raids were led by a chief named Victorio, who was driven by sheer despair to take the warpath and who proved as brilliant a leader as Crazy Horse.

The Army had an impossible task. The Southwest was riddled with corrupt officials who made fortunes out of the Indians, buying rotten food for them and pocketing money meant for them. Many traders encouraged Indian atrocity stories so as to bring in more troops—and more trade for them. Also, by helping promote Indian wars there was always a chance of grabbing more Indian land after the army had driven the renegades back to their shrinking reservations. Soon the best land would all be white. As for the government, far away in Washington, it had little idea of conditions on the spot and, even when it meant well, usually made matters worse.

But gradually, thanks to General Crook, a humane man and a brilliant Indian fighter who had the sense to use Apaches to catch Apaches, conditions improved and fewer Indians left on raids.

Dutchy, one of the fiercest of Apache scouts, who enlisted with the Americans to track down hostiles. When the wars were over he was sent to a Florida prison camp along with the hostiles (Smithsonian Institution, National Anthropological Archives)

Even the most famous of the later chiefs, Geronimo, seemed content to stay put much of the time. But in March 1886 a drink-peddlar called Tribolett went to work. He may have been hired by the crooked Americans who wanted another war badly, but whatever the reason, he filled Geronimo and his band not only with rot-gut whisky, but with alarming stories of what would happen if they returned to the reservation for good. The whites would surely hang them, said this unsavoury character, and soon Geronimo, Cochise's son Naiche, twenty other warriors, thirteen women and six children were riding hell-bent for the border to escape into the vastnesses of the Sierra Madre Mountains of Mexico.

General Crook, who had offered Geronimo the best possible terms for surrendering after his last outbreak, had had enough, especially when General Sheridan, the head of the army, questioned his way of running things and insultingly suggested that his Apache scouts could not be trusted. He resigned, and into Arizona came General Miles.

The last two Apache leaders (on horseback) Geronimo (left) and Naiche, son of Cochise. Standing at Geronimo's side is one of his sons (National Archives)

Nelson A. Miles, ambitious and able finished off the Apache Wars. He selected a band of men to act as a flying column, ready to ride anywhere at any time, and he used heliographs—mirrors for flashing Morse messages—to send information from hill to hill. He even used some Apache scouts. But he disgraced himself by rounding up peaceful Apaches and sending many of them to a Florida prison camp, then surpassed himself by sending Crook's loyal scouts there as well. It was one thing to send Geronimo and his band there when they finally gave up in September 1886, but to send men who had served against him and earlier renegades was infamous.

Only the non-stop efforts of General Crook and a few other well-wishers prevented the surviving Apaches in their humid unhealthy prison camp from dying to a man. They were moved to Alabama, next to Indian Territory. Then, in 1907, those who wanted to were allowed to settle with the Mescalero Apaches in New Mexico. No Chiricahua was allowed back to Arizona. Old Geronimo died in 1909 at Fort Sill in what by then was Oklahoma.

The True American

Let us end this chapter with two quotations. The first was written by a white cowboy named Charles Russell who became a friend of the Indians, as well as being a magnificent artist of the Western scene.

> The Red man was the true American. They have almost all gone, but will never be forgotten. The history of how they fought for their country is written in blood, a stain that time cannot grind out. Their God was the sun, their church all out doors. Their only book was nature and they knew all the pages.

But the Red Man has not vanished, for all his terrible problems as he strives to hold onto something of his old life, sometimes on reservations bleak beyond belief. Some Indians prosper away from the reservations, some, the majority, do not; some have transformed their reservations into paying propositions, others have found oil on theirs, others even now have to fight to retain them, fighting in law-courts, not on the warpath. The Apaches, not surprisingly, do not take to farming but make fine cowboys.

Here is our second quotation, spoken by Chief Dull Knife of the Northern Cheyennes, who in 1878 led his people on an epic fighting march towards their old homeland, a march on which most of them died:

> All we ask is to be allowed to live, and live in peace . . . We bowed to the will of the Great Father and went south. There we found a Cheyenne cannot live. So we came home. Better it was, we thought, to die fighting than to perish of sickness. . . . You may kill me here; but you cannot make me go back. We will not go. The only way to get us there is to come in here with

John F. Clum tried to rule the Apaches on the grim San Carlos Reservation with kindness as well as firmness, much to the displeasure of most white Arizonans (National Archives)

clubs and knock us on the head, and drag us out and take us down there dead.

Just a few of the uses of the buffalo

Rawhide (untreated skin) was used for stirrup coverings, picket ropes, horseshoes, moccasin soles etc.

Hide (made soft and pliable by tanning) was used for leggings, moccasins, breechcloths, tipi covers, door flaps and linings—cow hide was used for these last three and horse blankets, saddle blankets etc.

Bone was used for arrowheads, knives, sewing awls, dice etc.

Horns were used for powder flasks, ladles, cups etc.

Hair was used for tipi ornaments (plus the tail), headdress ornaments (plus horns), bridles (plus rawhide) etc.

Glue came from hide and hooves, water buckets from the paunch, soap from fat and berry bags from the hide of an unborn calf.

This list could be twice as long. Most of the work on the buffalo, the actual killing apart, was done by women of the tribe.

Sitting Bull, Sioux warrior and medicine man (Smithsonian Institution, National Anthropoligical Archives)

What was Indian medicine and who was the medicine man?
Medicine is not easy to explain, but it was the Indian's spirit protection, his 'charm', even his luck.

As for the medicine man, or shaman, his duties varied from tribe to tribe. Sometimes his main duties were ceremonial, and he was expected to prophesy, as Sitting Bull (a medicine man as well as a war chief) did on occasion.

But many medicine men were more concerned with healing, which was not simply a matter of chanting, or beating drums. Down the centuries much medical knowledge had been acquired, some of it far in advance of that of the white men. The basic facts about penicillin were understood by Indians long before white men used it, and no less than 170 Indian drugs have been accepted by American experts. Of course, many Indian remedies were useless, like white medicines of the same period, but many a white man owed his life to Indian skills.

How did Indians get their names?
First let it be noted that we know their names only in (often bad) translations. For instance, 'Young Man Afraid of his Horses' was not a coward. His name probably meant that he was so great a warrior that even his horses inspired fear. And 'Rain in the face' meant 'His face is like a storm.'

Indians often had more than one name during their lifetime. The first was given at birth, usually by a relation or medicine man. It might be an ancestor's name, or recall a brave act by the donor of the name, or, perhaps, commemorate a flash of lightning at birth, or a personal characteristic. Most women kept their birth name, but men later took a new one, from a vision, perhaps, or a daring deed, or even an animal. Sitting Bull started life as Slow, getting his famous later name after a brave deed in battle when he was still a boy. He touched an enemy with his 'coup stick' in the most daring way. The enemy was facing him on foot with an arrow in his bowstring. Slow galloped up towards him, touched him with the stick, spoiled his aim, and galloped away again, his horse having knocked the Indian flat before turning. That evening Slow's father hailed him in front of the Sioux, as the boy sat on his horse, daubed from head to foot in the black paint of victory. 'I name him *Tananka Yotanka*, Sitting Bull,' said the proud father.

What happened to Indian Territory?

Like most Indian lands, it was meant to be the property of the red men for ever, but legal land grabs with government blessing began with a frantic rush in 1889. The town of Guthrie sprang from nothing to 10,000 people in an afternoon. The Territory became Oklahoma in 1907, and the last Rush occurred in 1911. Happily, Indians in Oklahoma today play a fuller part in the life of their state than do Indians anywhere else in the United States.

On September 16, 1893, 100,000 men, women and children poured into the Cherokee Outlet, Indian Territory, with the Government's blessing. It was the biggest of all the land rushes to settle the Last Frontier (Oklahoma Historical Society)

The faces of defeat. Captive Bannack Indians, 1870 (Montana Historical Society)

THINGS TO JOIN,
READ AND SEE

There is only one organisation in Britain devoted entirely to the study of the American West and that is the English Westerners' Society. Its publications range in subject matter from Jesse James to Geronimo, from the Mountain Men to the Mandan Indians, from book reviews to an exchange and mart section. Details can be got from the Secretary, English Westerners' Society, 29 The Tinings, Monkton Park, Chippenham, Wilts.

In the United States, State Historical Societies are usually most helpful in giving information, and copies of early photographs can be bought from them at reasonable prices. Addresses can be obtained from the American Embassy, Grosvenor Square, London W1.

The leading museums in Britain have a certain number of Indian relics on display, including the British Museum in London. The Horniman Museum, London Road, London SE 23, takes a special interest in the West. A must for young and old is the American Museum at Claverton Manor, near Bath, where history is brought to life in a most exciting way.

Western magazines published in the States are not usually very accurate, and madden those who want the facts. Exceptions are those published by Western Publications Inc., P.O. Box 3338, 1012 Edgecliff Terrace, Austin, Texas 78764 U.S.A., whose magazines, **True West, Frontier Times** and **Old West,** are far ahead of their rivals.

Most public libraries stock some books on the West. Currently, Time-Life Books are bringing out a most exciting series of lavishly illustrated books which will appeal even to the youngest Westerners. Published in Britain, titles include **The Indians, The Pioneers, The Cowboys, The Gunfighters, The Forty-Niners, The Railroaders, The Soldiers,** and **The Trailblazers.**

Here is a short list of books usually obtainable in Britain and worth everyone's attention:

The American Heritage Book of Indians (Eyre and Spottiswoode).
Pictorial History of the American Indian by Oliver La Farge

(Spring Books).

The Truth about Geronimo by Britton Davis (Yale).

Six Years with the Texas Rangers by James Gillett (Yale).

They Called Him Wild Bill by Joseph G. Rosa (University of Oklahoma Press).

The Vigilantes of Montana by Thomas Dimsdale (University of Oklahoma Press).

Klondike by Pierre Berton (W. H. Allen).

And the following works of fiction:

Blood Brother by Elliott Arnold (Eyre and Spottiswoode). This is about Cochise and Tom Jeffords and is one of the best historical novels ever written about the West.

The Way West by A. B. Guthrie (Four Square), about the Oregon Trail.

Shane by Jack Schaeffer, all of whose books and stories are far ahead of most Western fiction.

Not all these books are in print at any given moment, but your public library will try to get any of them for you.

Real Western fans tend to look down at Westerns made for television. They are so much *softer* than the actual West. Films are often liable to picture the West in a romantic glow, but no keen Westerners will miss a good Western if he or she can help it. And luckily plenty of good ones are shown on television. Here is a short list of Westerns which stand out, with apologies if favourite ones, including silent classics, are omitted:

Stagecoach (1939), directed by John Ford. The first great sound Western.

Red River (1948), directed by Howard Hawks. Up the trail to Kansas with John Wayne and hundreds of cattle.

She Wore a Yellow Ribbon (1949), directed by John Ford. A marvellous U.S. Cavalry picture, starring John Wayne.

Broken Arrow (1950), directed by Delmer Daves. Not as good as the novel which inspired it **(Blood Brother,** see above), but the first modern film to give the Indian point of view strongly. Jeff Chandler as Cochise and James Stewart as Tom Jeffords.

High Noon (1952), directed by Fred Zimmermann. A classic starring Gary Cooper.

Shane (1953), directed by George Stevens. It is a little romantic perhaps—no Western looks more beautiful—but one of the supreme Westerns, sticking closely to the book (see above), which was partly inspired by Wyoming's Johnson County War.

Apache (1954), directed by Robert Aldrich. Tough and, thanks to Burt Lancaster, more believable than most Indian films starring a browned-up paleface.

The Searchers (1956), directed by John Ford, and one of his best.

The Big Country (1958), directed by William Wyler.

Butch Cassidy and the Sundance Kid (1969), directed by George Roy Hill. For all the comedy and tricks, it was true to the naughty pair.

Jeremiah Johnson (1972), directed by Sydney Pollack and starring Robert Redford. The only first-rate Mountain Man movie.

ACKNOWLEDGEMENTS

Finally, a brief word of thanks to three fellow English Westerners Jeff Burton, Allan Radbourne and Joseph Rosa, for friendly advice, and to the many Americans who go out of their way to help British students of their wonderful Old West, particularly Katherine Halverson of the Wyoming State Historical Society, who showed me Fort Laramie and the Oregon Trail wagon ruts, Joe Snell of the Kansas State Historical Society, Andrew Rolle, Tim Bannon, Fredie Steve Harris and Richard Dillon, also the Wells Fargo Bank History Room ladies.

INDEX